*on t*

# Emerson, Lake & Palmer

every album, every song

Mike Goode

Sonicbond Publishing Limited
www.sonicbondpublishing.co.uk
Email: info@sonicbondpublishing.co.uk

First Published in the United Kingdom 2019
First Published in the United States 2019

British Library Cataloguing in Publication Data:
A Catalogue record for this book is available from the British Library

Typset in ITC Garamond & Berthold Akzidenz Grotesk
Printed and bound in England

Graphic design and typesetting: Full Moon Media

# *on track ...*
# Emerson, Lake & Palmer

every album, every song

Mike Goode

SONICBOND PUBLISHING

sonicbondpublishing.co.uk

# on track...
# Emerson, Lake & Palmer

every album, every song

Mike Goode

# With Thanks

The writing of this book was way more difficult than I ever imagined. When I happily volunteered to write it for Stephen Lambe, Managing Director at Sonicbond Publishing, I had no idea of the road immediately ahead. How could anyone possibly know that in a very short while I'd have upped sticks from where I was living in the south-east of England, to return home to Wales to be closer to my Mother who had been diagnosed with Motor Neurone Disease. I am writing this just three months short of the day she passed away, finally at peace. Mum knew I was writing this book and wished me all the best with its publication. It is to her memory this book is dedicated.

It is only fitting that Dad also gets a tip of the hat. Whereas Mum probably wouldn't have recognised any ELP if she heard it – maybe aside from Greg Lake's Christmas single – Dad most certainly would. I once even 'caught' him playing one of my ELP albums on his beloved Sony music centre! A lover of big band jazz, he immediately recognised that Carl Palmer's drumming owed much to the style of jazz drumming legend Buddy Rich. He was right, it does. At the time I didn't even know who Buddy Rich was. Years later, Dad even accompanied me to a Carl Palmer drum clinic, enjoying the flamboyant demonstration as much as any of the ELP fans in attendance. Dad, who passed away a couple of years before Mum, this is for you too.

Thanks must also go to my wife Laura, who graciously gave me the time and space needed to complete this book. Most of the words were written in the kitchen of our new house in Wales, the rest of the building in absolute turmoil as builders and tradesmen of every description generated enough dust to create a weather warning across the entire South Wales region. I kid you not. Thankfully, as I type these words, most of the building work has been done. I can finally look forward to the day when my mancave is once more graced by the many ELP albums and band-related ephemera that has been living on our kitchen table for months. The question is, when I finally put it all back on the shelves, should I order alphabetically or chronologically?

In creating this book, of all the fellow ELP fans, former roadies and associates who have contributed with their memories, I must give a big heartfelt thank you to the artist and designer William Neal. William, who worked on the *Tarkus*, *Pictures at an Exhibition* and *Trilogy* album covers, graciously gave me a lot of his time in retelling the stories from his days working with the band. It was heartwarming to hear the high regard in which he holds Keith Emerson, Greg Lake and Carl Palmer.

And without all three, there would of course be no albums and therefore no book. I therefore thank each of them individually, and as a band, for enriching our lives with the music they created. Although we have lost both Keith and Greg in recent years, ELP's musical heritage lives on.

Lastly, a very special thanks to you for buying this book. I hope that my passion for all-things ELP is passed on and that you too become similarly enthused. Assuming of course that you're not already afflicted!

# on track ...
# Emerson, Lake & Palmer

## Contents

# Foreword (it has never been cool to like ELP)

The full blame for this book rests squarely on the shoulders of Steve Lewis. It is his fault. Although Steve, of course, will blame his older cousin. Perhaps I should explain.

In the dim and distant Seventies, Steve and I were at school together. The very same school that years later would produce Gareth Bale, Sam Warburton and Geraint Thomas. As far as I am aware, there is zero connection between ELP and said sporting heroes, so why I tell you all this I'm not sure.

More relevant is the fact that Steve's dad was into hi-fi. And it was on said hi-fi that Steve played me an album his cousin had recommended to him – a first pressing of *Pictures at an Exhibition*. The combination of ELP and hi-fi was potent. I have to say, if I'm being totally honest, that I'm not sure the effect would have been quite the same if *Pictures* had been played on my Mum's Dansette. So Steve's dad deserves credit for his part in all this. Thanks Mr Lewis!

For me, it was a Eureka! moment, the point at which there was no looking back to Slade and The Sweet of a few months earlier. My world had exploded in a cacophony of synthesisers, prog symphony and science fiction. I had never heard of a Moog synthesiser so the unearthly sounds coming from the hi-fi were a complete mystery. As for who Keith Emerson, Greg Lake or Carl Palmer were, I had no idea. In fact, for a while afterwards I assumed they were American. It was only later I discovered their pedigree and the fantastic bands they sprung from.

One thing was very quickly evident. Being into ELP was not cool. It would get even worse before the end of the decade but even in the mid-'70s writing ELP on your school satchel would be unlikely to gain you a knowing nod from the playground cognoscenti. And it goes without saying that carrying an ELP album under your arm was extremely unlikely to gain admiring glances from girls. In fact, carrying any prog album was the equivalent of wearing an invisibility cloak in that respect. This you probably already know.

Smitten, Steve and I went on the hunt for further ELP albums. We eventually plucked up the courage to enter the dark caverns that masqueraded as Cardiff record shops at that time, quickly discovering *Tarkus* and *Trilogy* – both of which I taped from Steve. Ample evidence, your honour, that the 'home taping is killing music' campaign was beyond daft. In fact, today I must own at least half a dozen copies of each album. Probably more.

By the time we'd familiarised ourselves with the rest of ELP's back catalogue and had started sniffing around The Nice, King Crimson and Atomic Rooster, I'd already fallen a long way down the rabbit hole of prog and classic rock. This is mainly thanks to enlightenment at the altar of Alan Freeman's legendary *Saturday Rock Show*. Not arf!

I soon realised there was not, and never has been, another band like ELP. They were, and are, totally unique. And despite brief dalliances with other bands – and even other genres – it is ELP who I've returned to again and again. Their music conjures something deep within me that words alone cannot hope to describe. Sure, part of it is nostalgia, but part of it is also a recognition of a time when rock music was at its peak. Has the musicianship, songwriting and creative use of technology from those times ever been bettered? I don't think it has.

Punk came and went, only briefly tempering my ELP obsession. Then, in the late-80s, I found myself working for IPC Magazines, the publisher of Melody Maker and the NME. Given a free run of the archives, I became acutely aware that the files marked ELP were getting increasingly dusty and looking forlorn. I think that was the moment I knew I had to do something. Although admittedly it has taken me a while!

The chance to write and compile this book is thanks to Stephen Lambe. If ever there was someone who deserves an award for services to prog and classic rock, Stephen is the man. It is his day job as a publisher than has resulted in this book, but his passion as a music fan that brought us together. I hope you enjoy this attempt to convey my years of ELP knowledge and hope it furthers your knowledge of all things ELP, but more than anything else, I hope it enhances your enjoyment of the music they produced.

Mike Goode, September 2018

# By Way of an Introduction (From the Beginning)

This book is not intended to be a comprehensive history of Emerson, Lake & Palmer (hereafter written as simply ELP) and their solo careers. It does, however, detail every known studio track the band ever recorded – starting with ELP's debut release and continuing until their last studio album, *In The Hot Seat*. As well as the author's personal comments and opinion on each track, included are details on the band's recording sessions and any alternative studio versions. Where relevant, information on the band's live performances of the track in question have also been mentioned.

If any new information comes to light that supersedes some of what is written in this book, the author politely asks the reader to forgive any such oversights. First and foremost a fan, the author further requests to be informed of any such information, believing it is paramount that all information on ELP and their recorded legacy be as accurate as possible. All opinion, it goes without saying, is the author's own.

# Emerson, Lake & Palmer (1970)

Personnel:
Keith Emerson: Hammond organ, piano, Moog synthesiser IC
Greg Lake: vocals, bass, acoustic guitar, electric guitar
Carl Palmer: drums & percussion
Released: 20 November 1970 (UK), 1 January 1971 (USA)
Recorded: Advision Studios, London, July 1970
Highest chart place: 4 in UK, 18 US Billboard 200

When ELP got together in the Summer of 1970, they spent time rehearsing, both in preparation for gigs and recording their much anticipated debut album. The new band was quickly dubbed a supergroup – a tag they intensely disliked. Although Greg Lake had won plaudits for his role as the vocalist and bassist on King Crimson's *In the Court of the Crimson King*, most of the attention was on Keith Emerson. His previous band, The Nice, had been a huge concert draw – although album sales had arguably not met record company expectations. By hooking up with Lake, who was a more accomplished singer and bass player than The Nice's Lee Jackson, Emerson knew that the sky was the limit for his musical ambitions.

After holding auditions for a drummer, Emerson and Lake settled on Carl Palmer, then playing with Atomic Rooster, but formerly of The Crazy World of Arthur Brown. Although Palmer was initially reluctant to join – mainly because the new venture was such an unknown quantity – he was eventually convinced by their passionate vision and the undeniable musical chemistry when all three jammed together. According to Melody Maker's Chris Welch, who helped champion the new band, they'd only played together four times when the journalist was invited to meet them at their rehearsal space – a church hall in Notting Hill, London. Despite Emerson and Lake's more illustrious pedigree, it was evident to Welch that Palmer was being treated as an equal and was already eagerly contributing ideas. In fact, it was as a result of Palmer's suggestion that the band tackled an arrangement of Bartok's *Allegro Barbaro* – a piece that became 'The Barbarian', the opening track on the new album.

Although briefly considering Triton as a name, they decided to call themselves Emerson, Lake & Palmer, to signal the fact they were all equal partners and to help take away the focus from Emerson. Lake, in particular, was keen that the new band not be seen as The Nice 'mark two'. His one concession was in agreeing to play 'Rondo', a piece Emerson had promised The Nice fans he would continue to play in his new band. Initially, they also rehearsed King Crimson's '21st Century Schizoid Man'. However, neither were intended for the new album. In the end, '21st Century Schizoid Man' didn't even make it into the live set.

By the time they entered Advision Studios in July 1970, ELP had rehearsed almost enough material for their debut album. Advision, as the name implies, had initially been conceived as a studio for commercial voice-overs for the advertising industry. Located at 23 Gosfield Street, in London's Fitztrovia, it featured a massive studio space – large enough to house a 60-piece orchestra. In the late '60s its central location helped make it popular with bands such as The Yardbirds and The Move. Then, in 1968, it became the very first studio in the UK to have an 8-track tape machine. With rock music in the ascendancy, a new wave of bands began using the studio – even more-so after a custom 24-channel mixing desk was installed in late 1970. Little wonder then that ELP were keen for a slice of the action. Their passion to embrace new technology became a constant across their entire career.

With Greg Lake taking the role of producer – something that Emerson frequently claimed was not a conscious democratic band decision – Eddy Offord was recruited as sound engineer. Offord has since, rather disparagingly, claimed that Advision was an outdated studio with an old mixing desk and very little in the way of outboard effects aside from an echo plate. This lack of fancy equipment may seem incredible to musicians today, but back then it was fairly normal in the UK. It was very different in the USA, where Offord later moved. Besides, a lack of 'bells and whistles' encouraged creative experimentation – something ELP were definitely not averse to. The band used the eight tracks available to them by recording live, keeping overdubs to a minimum. Despite Emerson's comments with regard to Lake seizing the production role, there were no criticisms about the quality of his work. He'd already gained invaluable production experience working on *In the Court of the Crimson King* – a role forced on King Crimson after the band had aborted sessions with The Moody Blues producer, Tony Clarke. At the helm for ELP, Lake learned fast, his teamwork with Offord resulting in an album that is full of vitality and high on audio quality.

The cover was designed by Nic Dartnell. Just 18 at the time, he was working in a record shop in Edinburgh, when his boss – who would later become Simple Minds' manager – sent the famous dove painting to Island Records in London. The painting obviously impressed as it was shown to ELP, who immediately chose it for their first album. Dartnell claims that, 'I didn't even know who ELP were at the time'! In many ways, it is a shame that UK and US releases of the album weren't given a gatefold sleeve to show Dartnell's painting to its best effect. That honour was only bestowed on the first pressing of the German issue – which is a rarity today.

## 'The Barbarian' (Bartok, arranged Emerson, Lake, Palmer)

Hearing Keith Emerson playing Bartok's *Allegro Barbaro* during an early rehearsal, Carl Palmer suggested they try arranging it for the band. This primeval slice of ELP is highly reminiscent of Atomic Rooster's debut album, particularly the fuzz bass intro and Palmer's dry drum sound. When combined with Emerson's distorted Hammond, the sound pleased fans of The Nice, especially when Emerson switched to piano and started tackling Bartok's composition in earnest.

The similarity to the original classical piece is strong, making the Hungarian composer's omission from the credits all the more baffling when the album was originally released. Emerson distanced himself from the furore by claiming writing credits were the role of the record company's publishing department and that he was simply the musician. Things came to a head when Bartok's disgruntled widow objected, furious that ELP had taken so many liberties with her beloved husband's composition. The situation was apparently not helped by the band renaming their adaptation 'The Barbarian'.

Bartok had written *Allegro Barbaro* as a piano piece in 1911. ELP's aggressive treatment must have been alien to the ears of Mrs Bartok, so little wonder she tried to sue for copyright. The band and their management backed down and apologised. As a result, later pressings of the album were given an amended label copyright, although oddly not on the rear sleeve. 'Adapted from Bela Bartok's *Allegro Barbaro* by Emerson Lake & Palmer' left little doubt as to the track's origins – and rightly so. Interestingly, when the CD copy of the album was issued, the original error was repeated and Bartok's name was again nowhere to be seen. The latest CD issues have rectified the situation with a less-wordy 'Bartok, arranged Emerson, Lake, Palmer'.

Intriguingly, 'The Barbarian' was omitted from any ELP compilation until 2007's *The Essential Emerson, Lake & Palmer*. This is a shame as it is one of the band's earliest defining moments. It obviously wasn't considered a prime example of quintessential ELP by compilers, although most ELP fans would heartily disagree. As would the band themselves because 'The Barbarian' was in their set from the off – including their show at the Isle of Wight Festival on Saturday 29 August 1970, only their second gig. Such was the power and impact of 'The Barbarian' when played live, it was given pride of place as the opening number during their first two UK tours, including ELP's first excursion to the USA, between April and May 1971. It stayed in the set until usurped by a new opener, 'Hoedown', from their third UK tour onwards. 'The Barbarian's' last live appearance, fittingly, was at ELP's last ever gig at London's High Voltage Rock Festival in 2010. It features on both the DVD and CD issues of that gig. 'The Barbarian' makes just one appearance on ELP's *Original Bootleg Series* – the four boxes of live recordings that proudly sits astride virtually their entire career – on *Volume One*, recorded at the band's Gaelic Park gig on 1 September 1971. This is the concert experienced by none other than Bob Moog, who described the scenes as 'biblical'. It was the first time he'd see Emerson play one of his synthesisers live – a seminal moment.

## 'Take a Pebble' (Lake)
Composed on an acoustic guitar, 'Take A Pebble' was one of the handful of songs played to Melody Maker journalist Chris Welch at an early rehearsal.

What ELP fan wouldn't have sold their grandmother to be in attendance that day? In his own words, They played a beautiful number called 'Pebbles', which sounded like a rock version of the Modern Jazz Quartet, with Carl on brushes, Keith on piano and Greg singing in a rich, warm style'.

Lake later said that he developed 'Take A Pebble' from a guitar line he wrote while in The Shame, one of his earliest bands. He is believed to have played the song to an unimpressed Robert Fripp for inclusion on King Crimson's debut. Emerson, however, saw potential in the song, taking its bare bones and turning it inside out – a mark of the pioneering creativity that typifies ELP's 'golden era' of the early 1970s. Be honest, how many of us guessed that 'Take A Pebble' was originally an acoustic guitar number? Instead of Lake's delicately picked guitar intro, Emerson holds down the keys on his piano while strumming the strings inside using a guitar plectrum – a sound that intrigued when the album was first released. Joined by Lake's deep resonant bass and with delicate cymbal work from Palmer, the entire first section of 'Take A Pebble' is one of ELP's most refined moments. When Lake begins singing, backed by Emerson's improvised piano, it sets the scene for over twelve minutes of some of the most varied and creative music the band ever played. Their subtle playing is light years away from the pomp and bombast they later became renowned for. For many, 'Take A Pebble' is the ultimate example of ELP working together as a band, leaving one to wonder why they didn't attempt to repeat this beguiling formula on future albums.

Eventually, the focus on Emerson's piano switches to Lake's acoustic guitar, finally giving hints of how the song might originally have sounded. Partly improvised, Lake's accurate and highly musical picking on his beloved Gibson J-200 is interspersed with the atmospheric sound of water droplets – generated on Emerson's Moog. After the tempo suddenly picks up for a brief country-tinged strummed section, complete with handclaps, for the first time on an ELP album we're treated to some accomplished cross-picking and use of guitar harmonics from Lake. Both would become one of his much-loved trademarks.

After six minutes or so, the piano reintroduces itself, Lake's sparse bass beautifully complementing Emerson's accomplished keyboard work. When Palmer joins in, Lake's jazzy bass runs add colour and the track increases in intensity. At just shy of eleven minutes of this ambitious work, the original theme is revisited, Lake's double tracked refrain, 'of our lives' sung over Emerson's cascading piano as the track ends in an understated but confident manner. The chemistry between the three musicians is a joy to hear, 'Take A Pebble' unlike anything from their former bands and pretty much unlike anything any other progressive rock band ever attempted. This is contemporary progressive rock at its finest.

'Take A Pebble' became a mainstay of the band's live set and was played at all of ELP's early gigs, including the Isle of Wight Festival, a performance captured on *Live at the Isle of Wight Festival 1970* CD. A mark of the importance of the piece to ELP is that it isn't easy to find a record of any gig they played that didn't include it. What is also worth noting is that ELP's live performance of the song changed dramatically over the years. In its earliest incarnation, Lake would use the quieter folk-guitar middle section to sing and play short snippets of other songs – such as the folk standard 'Old Blue'. For an example of the deep well that Lake drew upon in the early days of ELP, fans should listen and compare his rendition to the Byrds version on *Dr. Byrds & Mr. Hyde*. Lake would also use 'Take A Pebble' to sing some of his own acoustic numbers, notably 'Lucky Man' and 'Still…You Turn Me On'.

Not to be left out, Emerson used 'Take A Pebble' as a vehicle to play a wide variety of solo piano pieces and medleys. At times, listening back to ELP playing 'Take A Pebble' live, one gets the strong impression that Emerson had no idea what he was going to play until the moment was upon on him! This lends the piece an incredible amount of vitality and bears repeated listens of the many live examples in existence. On the four box sets that make up *The Original Bootleg Series*, 'Take A Pebble' features no less than eleven times! In later years, Emerson's piano section was shortened considerably and Lake's acoustic section was dropped entirely – mainly because his acoustic songs began to be played in their own right.

It is worth noting that the 2012 Steven Wilson reissue of *Emerson, Lake & Palmer* features an interesting alternate take. On the recording you can hear the band chatting before the song starts, Palmer encouraging the band with an enthusiastic 'yeah let's do one man, I feel like it'! The vitality is infectious as the band launch into a three minute and 40 second instrumental run through of the first part of 'Take a Pebble'.

An excellent DVD of the band playing 'Take A Pebble' in their early days is on the *Masters From The Vaults* DVD – filmed at their Zurich gig on 4 December 1970 – originally broadcast on Belgian TV. Although this isn't an official release, it perfectly captures the band's early spirit and virtuosity, making it essential viewing for any ELP fan.

## 'Knife Edge' (Janceck & Bach, arranged Emerson, lyrics by Lake & Fraser)

As with 'The Barbarian', the original credits for this track got ELP into deep trouble as they omitted both Janáček and Bach. There is no excuse as the song is largely based on the opening *Allegretto* fanfare of the Czech-born Leoš Janáček's *Sinfonietta*. Composed in 1926 for brass and percussion, ELP's adaptation takes the main theme as the vocal melody, with added dystopian lyrics by Lake and Fraser. The Fraser here is Dik Fraser, one of Kind Crimson's original roadies. He gets a writing credit for assisting Lake with the lyrics. Fraser later became ELP's tour manager.

'Knife Edge is one of the more immediate songs on *Emerson, Lake & Palmer*, its strident rock approach making it a popular live number. Angry, dark and heavy, the track sets the mood for much of ELP's early-70s output, its sci-fi theme in perfect tune with the times. Emerson's powerful Hammond organ playing, underpinned by Lake's half-speed bass and Palmer's hyperactive drumming, propels the track towards a startling conclusion. Evidence that the band were as creative during the mixing as they were when playing.

The Bach writing credit is due to Emerson's improvised quotation from the German composer's *French Suite* – heard just after three minutes and 20 seconds. By the time *Emerson, Lake & Palmer* was released on the band's own Manticore label in 1973, Janáček had gained a credit but not Bach – a neglectful situation carried over into the CD era. The situation has only relatively been rectified, finally giving both Janceck and Bach the credits they are due.

Steven Wilson's 'deluxe' edition of *Emerson, Lake & Palmer* includes a fascinating remix that omits the 'slowing down' effect on the tail-out of the original track. This had originally been achieved by manually restricting the speed of the tape when the track was mixed. Rather amusingly, it is an effect impossible to achieve digitally! Thanks to Wilson, on the 'deluxe' edition we get to hear the band play on for another minute or so, Emerson torturing his Hammond as the track peters out. As an extra bonus, Wilson also unearthed a previously unheard second version of 'Knife Edge' on the studio's master tapes. Although unfinished (the track has no vocals), it is fascinating to hear, the track ending soon after Emerson's Bach quotation as he hits a sustained chord on his trusty Hammond.

'Knife Edge' was a staple of the band's early gigs but was dropped when ELP toured in support of *Trilogy*. It was revived in 1977, making an appearance in the set backed by the ill-fated 70 piece orchestra. Emerson announced the song at their Madison Square Garden gig on 8 July 1997 with, 'This is something we had a lot of requests to do, so we dug it up again and re-arranged it'. A live version with the orchestra appears on the original vinyl issue of *In Concert*, recorded on 26 August 1977 at Montreal's Olympic Stadium. This gig was reissued, as an expanded set, as *Works Live* in 1993. In 2013 it was released again, with additional tracks, as *Live in Montreal 1977*. 'Knife Edge' appears on all three releases.

When the band reformed in the early-90s, 'Knife Edge' once again became a staple of the band's live performances. It appears on *Live at the Albert Hall*, *Live in Poland*, *Then & Now*, *High Voltage Festival* and *Live at Montreux 1997*.

## 'The Three Fates' (Emerson)

Side two of the original vinyl album opens with 'The Three Fates', a mini suite consisting of three movements. Based on Greek mythology, 'The Fates' are sometimes mentioned as the daughters of Zeus and Themis – or in older myths as the daughters of Nyx. The myths commonly portray them as spinners, each Fate being given a different task. Clotho spun the thread of life, while Lachesis measured its length and Atropos cut the cloth with her shears. Sometimes, however, each Fate was associated with time – Clotho was the present, Lachesis was the future and Atropos was the past.

ELP's 'The Three Fates' opens with 'Clotho', with Emerson on The Royal

Festival Hall's powerful four-manual pipe organ. The piece confidently surges from organ fanfares to more considered delicate passages, before Emerson switches to piano for the free-flowing 'Lachesis'. One of Emerson's most mature studio performances, 'Lachesis' is totally free of the indulgences and embellishment that sometimes clouds his later work. As Emerson's piano briefly gives way to a second blast of pipe organ, Palmer joins in for 'Atropos', the final movement. 'Atropos' works its way to an explosive conclusion (literally!), Emerson playing in an atonal manner, initially in 7/8 before the piece resolves in 4/4. The piano here sounds uncannily like a Caribbean steel drum ensemble – albeit one playing jazz! It is a supremely confident and eclectic statement. Perhaps tellingly, 'The Three Fates' never made the transition to the band's live set.

Steven Wilson's 'alternative ELP' disc, from the 2012 'deluxe' set, includes a different version of 'Atropos'. Marginally slower and less intense, Emerson seemingly hesitates as he improvises. Nevertheless, it provides excellent insight into the track's genesis, Palmer's vibraslap percussion punctuating the complex piano and drum groove. And as with the original album version, this 'new' 'Atropos' ends with a studio-created explosion heavy with reverb. Sadly, when searching through the ELP studio archives, Wilson could not find similar alternatives for either 'Clotho' or 'Lachesis', so 'Atropos' stands alone.

## 'Tank' (Emerson, Palmer)

Created by Emerson as a vehicle for a Palmer drum solo, 'Tank' is notable for the first appearance on an ELP album of the iconic modular Moog synthesiser. Emerson often told the story that he was in a record shop when the assistant played him *Switched on Bach* by Walter Carlos. When looking at the sleeve he immediately noticed the Moog, 'a huge electronic contraption covered with knobs and cables and stuff'. Desperate to find out more, he discovered that Mike Vickers of Manfred Mann owned a similar Moog Series III. Borrowing it for a concert at the Royal Festival Hall – with Vickers in attendance behind the scenes, pulling and plugging in the Moog's 'telephone exchange' of cables – Emerson remembers he could barely control the huge beast but managed to eke out excerpts from Stanley Kubrick's movie *2001* to impress fans! When ELP formed, Emerson knew he had to have his own Moog, so he wrote to inventor Bob Moog in the USA to order one. It arrived just in time to be included on *Emerson, Lake & Palmer*. It is said to have cost the majority of Emerson's advance from Island Records!

The first section of 'Tank' opens with a crisp drum groove – backed by lightly phased bass from Lake – before Emerson plays double-tracked piano and clavinet, panned hard left and right. With Lake's bass initially meandering behind the keyboards and Emerson effortlessly improvising, the two musicians suddenly lock together in unison, interspersed by Palmer's drum breaks. In Palmer's drum solo, facets of which he still employs to this day, he seemingly uses every item on his kit, including his famous gongs. Lake's production adds interest by phasing the sound, swirling the drums around the stereo mix. Back in the day, this was state-of-the-art, making ELP albums 'de rigueur' for hi-fi dealers to demonstrate their latest equipment. Although Palmer's solo is beautifully constructed and paced, one cannot help wonder how 'Tank' would have sounded with a far more concise demonstration of his undoubted percussive skills, letting the track stand on its own merits rather than as a vehicle for a solo. The thought obviously occurred to Palmer himself, as this is exactly what he did when re-recording the piece for *Works Volume 1*.

After the solo, the entire band rejoin Palmer, with clavinet, bass and drums laying down a solid, almost funky groove, with brassy layers of Moog laid over the top. The introduction of the Moog is an historic moment – the first time this ground-breaking instrument appears on an ELP album. Emerson's enthusiasm for the instrument adds a further dimension with a raspy improvised solo, Palmer's drumming getting ever more intense as the song races to its conclusion – not dissimilar to the effect later achieved on *Trilogy's* 'Abaddon's Bolero'.

In a live setting in the band's early days, 'Tank' was often inserted, minus the drum solo, into the improvised middle section of 'Take a Pebble'. Steven Wilson's 2012 reissue of *Emerson, Lake & Palmer* features an alternative take of the 'Tank' middle section – essentially, a different version of Palmer's drum solo. In this instance, Wilson allows us to hear the end section minus any phasing, allowing Palmer's Buddy Rich style beat to stand proudly on its own.

## 'Lucky Man' (Lake)

Lake often told the story that ELP had come to the end of recording their debut album but they were short of one track. He suggested trying an acoustic song he'd originally written when just twelve years old. After demoing the song and playing it to the band, Keith Emerson was apparently unsure what he could add to the track – or indeed whether it was suitable for inclusion – so he left Lake and Palmer to record it while he retired to the pub. On his return, Lake had added vocals, bass and electric guitar, fleshing out the sound. With Palmer's considered and creative drumming, the track had come alive, so Emerson agreed to try a Moog solo overdub at the end. With the tape running, he played an ad hoc solo and shouted to Lake, who was behind the mixing desk in the control room, that he was ready for a take. Lake replied that what he had just done was fine! Although Emerson insisted he could do better, he was convinced to come and hear what he'd just recorded. His improvised runs were left exactly as is – arguably the most famous Moog solo in music history!

'Lucky Man' was released as a single in 1970, reaching the top 20 in the Netherlands and charting in the USA (at number 48) and in Canada (at number 25). The song helped break ELP in the USA, although they didn't play the song live in its entirety for many years. Emerson said, 'It is a shame that we really can't perform it the same way it is on the album. There's a lot of double-tracked vocals and Greg's playing electric, bass and acoustic guitar. If we had really thought about it, we would have possibly re-arranged it so we could have done it on stage. Now we come out and people want to hear it, so Greg performs it as an acoustic piece. I guess it's rather disappointing to some people because they want to hear the recorded version.'

On the band's early tours, Lake would typically play 'Lucky Man' as part of his acoustic interlude in 'Take a Pebble', although it didn't regularly feature until their third North American tour in the Spring of 1972. Surprisingly, it wasn't until ELP reformed in the early '90s that 'Lucky Man' was played in its entirety, complete with Emerson's mighty Moog solo!

The Steven Wilson 2012 deluxe edition of *Emerson, Lake & Palmer* features two additional versions of 'Lucky Man'. The first is Greg Lake's initial demo, which Wilson mixed minus Palmer's drums. Lake claimed that Palmer's drum take was unsuccessful and although it survived on the master tape, Wilson sensibly omitted it so we can hear the bare bones of the song as he originally presented it to the rest of the band. It is fascinating to hear such a familiar song stripped back to just guitar, bass and vocals. The second version of 'Lucky Man' is an alternative mix, with Lake and Palmer laying down their respective parts live in the studio. In place of Emerson's Moog solo, Lake improvises a distorted guitar. It also differs in that there is no fade at the end, Wilson letting us hear everything on the tape, Lake's acoustic guitar simply petering out.

For such an iconic song, it is surprising there haven't been any significant cover versions. Tommy Shaw of Styx and Jack Blades of Night Ranger did a version on their *Influence* album, lead guitar taking the place of Emerson's Moog in what is otherwise a fairly authentic facsimile. A more interpretative country-tinged version, by Jim James, vocalist with My Morning Jacket, appeared on his *Tribute To 2* album in 2017. Perhaps most successful cover of all is the 2010 release by Welsh progressive rock band, Magenta. This was originally intended to appear on a Classic Rock magazine ELP tribute CD, to tie in with ELPs appearance at the High Voltage Festival. Sadly, the project was cancelled due to copyright problems, Magenta eventually deciding to release it themselves.

## *Emerson, Lake & Palmer* rarities and bonus tracks

2001 Sanctuary Records / Sanctuary Midline editions
Serial number: CMRCD165 / SMRCD055
Although these remastered editions contain no bonus tracks, they came with an informative twelve page fold-out booklet not present in other CD issues.

2012 deluxe edition
Serial numbers: Razor & Tie 7930183414-2 / Sony Music 88691937972 / Legacy 88691937972 / Manticore 88691937972 / Columbia 88691937972
The most definite release to-date are these 2012 issues. CD one is a remastered copy of the original album, whereas CD two features a new Steven Wilson

stereo mix, plus bonus tracks from the original studio sessions: 'Lucky Man' (with an extended outro), 'Promenade' (a studio version of the *Pictures at an Exhibition* track), 'Atropos' (an alternative version from 'The Three Fates'), 'Rave Up' (a fascinating jam, some of which would later manifest itself on *Tarkus*), a Carl Palmer drum solo (an outtake from 'Tank'), 'Take A Pebble' (an alternative version), 'Knife Edge' (an alternative version with no vocals) and two versions of 'Lucky Man' (the first Greg Lake demo and an alternative version). The DVD contains a new 5.1 surround sound mix by Steven Wilson of the original album, plus high-res stereo mixes of the bonus material. Also included is an informative booklet with notes from Wilson on the bonus tracks.

2013 vinyl edition
Serial number: MOVLP590
Spread across two albums, on 180g vinyl, this edition has the Steven Wilson remixes and bonus tracks from the 2012 CD issue. It includes a unique insert design but omits many of the notes on the CD booklet.

2014 Japanese limited edition
Serial number: VICP-78001
Issued in a 7 inch cardboard sleeve, this limited edition, remastered release is the original album plus 'The Barbarian' and 'Take A Pebble' from the Isle of Wight festival. The latter were later reissued as part of the band's entire set from the legendary festival.

2016 BMG Music Ltd
This release includes the original 2012 remastered album plus Steven Wilson 2015 stereo mixes and bonus tracks, but not the 5.1 surround sound mixes.

# Tarkus (1971)

Personnel:
Keith Emerson: Hammond organ, piano, Moog synthesiser IC
Greg Lake: vocals, bass, acoustic guitar, electric guitar
Carl Palmer: drums & percussion
Released: 14 June 1971 (UK), August 1971 (USA)
Recorded: Advision Studios, London, January 1971
Highest chart place: 1 in UK, 9 US Billboard 200

ELP's only number one album in the UK, *Tarkus* is renowned not only for its ambitious progressive music but also for its striking cover. The cover artist, William Neal, was central to the album's concept, working alongside the band to formulate the *Tarkus* story. His role in developing *Tarkus* cannot be overstated. Neil takes up the story, 'At the time I worked for CCS, a leading advertising agency for the music industry. Island Records formed part of our clientele. Apparently, ELP had problems in deciding on a suitable image for their second album and we were among many agencies asked to submit ideas. It happened by mistake that I had doodled a tiny armadillo with tank tracks on one of the artwork protection sheets while I was on the phone. It should never have slipped through to the presentation stage, but somehow it did.' Neal goes on to say that when the CCS team were presenting the ideas, Emerson noticed the doodle, became intrigued and asked to meet the artist. 'Keith felt he could work out more ideas along these lines, and the ideas I created evolved into a more sinister looking armadillo that Keith called *Tarkus*.'

The band were so pleased with the developing concept that Neal was given a copy of the music they were recording. Suitably inspired, the artist came up with other creatures, thus the *Tarkus* theme evolved. According to Neil, 'The door was open to all sorts of creatures. The Manticore was Keith's idea. In the end we ended up with too much material and a plethora of weird creatures had to be discarded'. Once the *Tarkus* idea was seized upon, work developed very quickly, the band's music and Neil's artwork taking around two weeks to complete. Where the *Tarkus* name came from, however, remains unclear. Emerson was quoted as saying he could have been unwittingly influenced by the name 'Tarka', from the *Tarka The Otter* story – an altogether gentler tale! However, he was aware that the theme the band were developing 'needed a science fiction name representing Darwin's theory of evolution in reverse – a mutation of the species caused by radiation'. William Neil is not so sure. He thinks the name could have come from 'Tartarus', the abyss beneath Hades in Greek mythology – an image that certainly better fits with the overall *Tarkus* theme of the futility of war.

It is interesting to learn that an early design for the album cover had the Tarkus creature on the back, with just its tail visible on the front. In the end, the band convinced Neil to redo the artwork, placing Tarkus proudly on the front. Emerson suggested spelling *Tarkus* in bones on the cover and with the design now so impactful, Neil convinced the band not to include their name on the design. It was a bold move, one that showed supreme confidence in the music they were creating, allowing the album to stand alone. Other bands of the era followed suit – notably, Led Zeppelin, who didn't even include a title on the cover of their November 1971 release – the album now commonly known as *Led Zeppelin IV*.

*Tarkus* was a pivotal moment in ELP's career. The ideas that Keith Emerson was developing using an unfinished piano manuscript given to him by Frank Zappa, together with the influence of Argentinian classical composer Albero Ginastera, hadn't gone down well with Greg Lake. He told Emerson, 'I can't play that kind of music. If that is what you want to play, then I think you should look for someone else'. Palmer was less confrontational. By coincidence he had been experimenting with different time signatures and had come up with a drum pattern in 5/4. Emerson took this unusual signature and fused it with the music he was developing. The result became 'Eruption', the album's opening track. The results encouraged Lake enough for the band to return to Advision Studios in London to begin recording. The album took around two weeks to complete. Initial recording sessions dealt with side one – the *Tarkus* concept – whereas side two was more diverse, from the dubiously-themed 'Jeremy Bender' to 'The Only Way', an anti-religious hymn.

*Tarkus* was released in the UK on 14 June 1971, and in the USA two months later. It impact was immediate. As well as hitting the number one spot in the UK, it stayed in the album charts for 17 weeks. In the USA, it reached number nine – only *Trilogy* climbing higher. Carl Palmer claims it was ELP's first true album, a real band effort. For Emerson it was a vindication not only of his compositional ambitions but also of his desire, as a keyboard player, to be seen on an equal footing as the guitar heroes of the day. In 1971's Melody Maker readers poll, ELP were given seven awards – a mark of their increasing popularity among rock fans. Even the music critics, for the most part, were positive.

ELP's new found popularity brought pressure for lengthy tours, especially in the USA. 'Tarkus', as a piece, was first performed on the band's second North American tour, between July and November 1971. Surprisingly, the only other track from *Tarkus to* feature it the set was 'A Time and a Place' – a number that was played only intermittently. On returning to the UK, ELP played 20 shows in 11 days, with 'Tarkus' taking over from *Pictures at an Exhibition* as the centrepiece of their set. 'A Time and a Place' was occasionally played as an encore, in place of 'Nutrocker'. 'Tarkus' would remain in ELP's set until their final performance.

Many fans recall ELP playing 'Tarkus' live, the stage flanked by two models of William Neal's fantastical creature. These produced smoke and fired foam-spewing guns into the crowd – accompanied by strobes and dramatic lighting. The two props were used for the first time at ELP's 30 September 1972 gig at the Melody Maker Poll Winners Concert at the Oval Cricket Ground in London.

Their use captured the public's imagination, even gaining favourable write-ups in the national press! They remained part of ELP's stage set-up for several tours – even when they were promoting *Trilogy* – becoming a part of ELP folklore.

## Side One:

The first side of the album is an entire suite based upon the *Tarkus* theme – a creature created by the band in conjunction with the artist William Neal. The inside of the album's gatefold sleeve illustrates the Tarkus story, from its birth inside a volcano, via battles with various biomechanical adversaries, to defeat at the hands of the Manticore. Blinded by the Manticore's scorpion-like tail, Tarkus retreats into the sea, to an unknown fate. Recorded in just six days, the music has impressive vitality and dynamics – the result of it being played live in the studio with minimal overdubs. That approach certainly paid dividends when ELP played 'Tarkus' live, the entire suite retaining its spirit and integrity. Although comments from band members on the nature of the concept are rare, Greg Lake gave an interview to the New Musical Express in February 1971, saying that the theme was broadly 'about the futility of conflict'.

The Tarkus creature is thought by some to represent the 'establishment' with links to power, money and war. In the aftermath of WWII, the 1960s brought brief hope – especially for the younger generation – and an attempt to reset man's ideals to 'make love, not war'. As the decade wore on, the hippy dream dissipated, corporate greed taking an ever-firmer grip on society. And with the horror of Vietnam and the Troubles in Northern Ireland always on the TV – coupled with Cold War threat of all-out nuclear war with the USSR – little wonder that musicians began to write about mankind's seemingly hellbent path to self-destruction. ELP set *Tarkus* in a post-apocalyptic world. The cover typography, written in bones beneath a human skull and animal skeletons, gives the impression that Tarkus had destroyed all before it and is now all-powerful. William Neal's cover design depicts Tarkus as a machine mercilessly killing its adversaries with ease... until it meets the Manticore.

## 'Eruption' (Emerson)

Developed from a piano idea inspired by the Argentine composer Alberto Ginastera, melded to a 5/4 drum pattern devised by Carl Palmer, 'Eruption' tells of the birth of Tarkus. Lake described 'Eruption' as being in a frustrating meter. This either an expression of his doubt at the music Emerson was writing at the time, or that the difficult time signature created a musical tension – or both! Despite Lake's initial reservations, as an introductory piece it grabs the listener's attention; Emerson's synth choir and Palmer's reversed cymbals – phased in the stereo image – acting as a platform to introduce Emerson's percussive Hammond-driven rhythm. With Moog fanfares and dramatic gongs announcing Tarkus' arrival, 'Eruption' certainly pulls no punches!

As well as Ginastera, Emerson also admitted to a Zappa influence when composing the music for *Tarkus*. 'I was a huge admirer of Frank Zappa and had met him on a few earlier occasions when he wanted my advice on how to cope with English orchestras. Frank was of the opinion that there shouldn't be time signatures. That's how I felt'. For 'Eruption', Emerson takes Zappa's opinion to heart. When rehearsing the material in preparation to record the album, ELP had many discussions on the time signatures they should be using. In the end, according to Emerson, 'Once Greg and Carl got the 5/4 down, and then we had the 10/8 section, everything else flowed.' He explained that because his bandmates didn't read music, they had to memorise it. 'Sometimes we rolled tape, just in case we got something worth keeping. We ran it down live as a trio, got a take, then we listened back in the control room for parts that needed overdubs.'

ELP's cuckoo-like tendency to borrow from other sources has long been criticised – something that irked Emerson. He claimed there was no attempt at outright plagiarism, merely that he was wearing his influences on his sleeve. In defending himself, he also admitted to a third influence on 'Eruption' – a fleeting one bar run from Prokofiev's *Third Piano Concerto in C* during the intro.

### 'Stones of Years' (Emerson, Lake)

At around 2 minutes 40 seconds, 'Eruption' merges into 'Stones of Years', the frantic pace of the intro slowing as Lake's lyrics question the stupidity of war. With deep resonant half-speed bass and Palmer's drums skipping nimbly around the languid groove, Emerson picks up the intensity with a dexterous Hammond solo. Lake's choirboy vocals lament the corrupt values that Tarkus represents. Exasperated, he sings, 'Are your ears full? You can't hear anything at all!' The song is a warning to mankind that ancient traditions and ways of life are under threat, all swept aside for power and money.

Virtually the whole of 'Tarkus' was completed when Emerson presented it to the band prior to recording – composed on an upright piano in his apartment in London and written out on manuscript. What was missing were songs and lyrics. Although Lake was initially unhappy with the direction the band were taking, he admirably knuckled down to turn two of Emerson's pieces, 'Stones of Years' and 'Mass', into songs. He also added a composition of his own, 'Battlefield'. The portentous lyrics on all three tracks, inspired by William Neal's artwork, are some of his best work, enhancing Emerson's compositions and helping 'Tarkus' to wider appeal.

### 'Iconoclast' (Emerson)

After 6 minutes 30 seconds, the pace increases, Palmer's furious tom-tom work laying a foundation for Emerson's gloriously in-your-face Hammond. A definition of an 'iconoclast' is a person who attacks or criticises long-held beliefs or institutions. ELP's 'Iconoclast' symbolises man's struggle against the establishment, only to fail and be destroyed. Emerson's composition is mechanical and angry – the fanfare towards the end of this short piece suggesting Tarkus has declared war on everything mankind holds dear.

## 'Mass' (Emerson, Lake)

Beginning with a funky Moog and guitar riff – both instruments playing in unison – 'Mass' is Lake's sarcastic take on the collusion between organised religion and governments. He makes no distinction between so-called democratic Western powers or communist regimes from the East. 'Mass' is the most varied piece in the 'Tarkus' suite, swinging between double-tracked vocal passages, and Emerson's classic percussive Hammond and Moog bursts, all interspersed by Lake's angular electric guitar playing. The lead guitar style here is very much a foretaste of his playing on *Brain Salad Surgery,* long sustained notes and melodic lines, showing a distinct Hank Marvin influence.

The Steven Wilson deluxe issue of *Tarkus,* from 2012, features an alternative instrumental version of 'Mass'. The is possibly an early take, as Emerson's percussive Hammond breaks sound less formulated and Lake's bass is not quite as assured. Regardless, it is a joy to hear how Palmer drives the track, his complex drumming managing to sound both colourful and powerful. Listening to this valuable ELP artefact, it is impossible to imagine any other drummer taking his role – a premise that would be challenged, with mixed results, when Emerson and Lake decided to team up with Cozy Powell in the mid-1980s.

## 'Manticore' (Emerson)

This fast paced Hammond, bass and drums workout has positive upbeat overtones, perhaps reflecting the confidence of the Manticore in facing Tarkus. The Manticore is the only creature from the *Tarkus* concept that wasn't created by ELP or William Neal. A mythical creature with ancient origins, the word Manticore means 'man-eater' in Persian, derived from the Latin 'mantichora'. The Manticore appeared an English heraldic device in around 1470, and in the 16th century was used as the badge of Robert Radcliffe, 1st Earl of Sussex. Whether there is a link here to Emerson's suggestion to use the Manticore as the 'hero' of the *Tarkus* album – bearing in mind he was living in Sussex at the time of the recording – is unknown.

Another mystery, something many ELP fans have wondered about, is how the Manticore in the ELP concept managed to avoid the might of Tarkus and get close enough to maim its eye – as shown in Neal's album cover illustration. Part lion, with a scorpion's tail and man's face, spines along the back of the Manticore could shoot poison arrows in any direction, although they'd likely be ineffective against the armour-plated Tarkus. We can perhaps surmise that the Manticore's voice, said to sound like pipes and trumpets, coupled with its trick of challenging prey with riddles, allowed it to get close enough to Tarkus to use its deadly sting. Neal's album cover illustration shows the Manticore facing down Tarkus before maiming it in the eye, so this seems a reasonable enough assumption – especially in light of the lack of any other explanation.

Of course, we can over-analyse these things – and do! Is it all just a story, or does the Manticore represent anything? Lake's 'Tarkus' lyrics suggest parallels between the mythical story William Neil illustrated and a number of themes

– notably including anti-war and protest. Perhaps the 'Manticore' stands for an alternative way of life and a return to simpler ideals? Or maybe we should simply take the track at face value and enjoy it as it is – a wonderful example of ELP at their very best.

## 'Battlefield' (Lake)

'Battlefield', the only track on side one not written with Emerson's involvement, tells the story of the aftermath of the duel between the two creatures. Lake's lyrics deal with the empty futility of a victorious battle, his guitar and vocals taking centre stage, reverb-soaked and anthemic. The guitar he used for the *Tarkus* sessions is believed to be a Fender Telecaster – an unusual choice for progressive rock. However, it was also the guitar of choice for Steve Howe on many of Yes' classic albums. Whether Lake was influenced by Steve Howe is unknown. Lake's Telecaster was customised with a hand-built maple neck and a Gibson humbucker in the neck pick-up position, presumably to give it a 'fatter' sound. Photographs show him using it on the *Tarkus* tour, but in an interview in Melody Maker he claimed he changed it for a stereo guitar – believed to be a semi-acoustic Gibson 345. Again, this is not an instrument Lake is usually associated with, so one can only guess that its stereo output is what attracted him. Photographs of him playing this rather exotic Gibson are rare, giving the impression that it too was soon swapped for another guitar – possibly a Les Paul, the guitar he was commonly seen with post-*Tarkus*.

## 'Aquatarkus' (Emerson)

On the album cover, the wounded *Tarkus* retreats into the sea. As hard as it is to crictise ELP's music on the album, this alone of the tracks on side one seems an afterthought. The music that accompanies the hellish creature's drive into the waves takes the form of a march, with Emerson's double-tracked Moog, unnervingly sounding like a kazoo, played over a rather uncertain backing. Lake and Palmer's parts seem improvised, almost not fully realised. Half way through, overdubbed onto the track, Palmer's snare drum beats a military tattoo. This rises in volume as Emerson's slightly aimless synth noodling gradually fades. One can of course forgive the band any slight blemishes to what is otherwise a faultless performance – and we need to bear in mind how fast *Tarkus* was written and recorded. In fact, in many ways, listening back to the sound of a band admirably 'winging it' in the studio only reinforces the impression of what great musicians they were!

   At the sound of one of Palmer's beloved gongs, the original 'Eruption' theme is re-introduced, redressing the balance after the slightly jokey-sounding 'Aquatarkus'. Finally, a series of brassy machine-like Moog stabs gives a fanfare. It is as if the Tarkus is saying 'you haven't seen the last of me, I'll be back', before Emerson's spiralling synths brings the entire dramatic suite to a close.

## Live notes

In a live setting, 'Tarkus' immediately became a cornerstone of the band's set – right up until their final performance. Famously, the live version on *Welcome Back My Friends* is around seven minutes longer! Energetically performed at a blistering pace, it is a massive testament to their collective musicianship that just three people could produce such a vast soundscape. The main reason for the longer running time on *Welcome Back My Friends* is an improvised section after 'Aquatarkus', Emerson playing some incredibly powerful Moog. The sounds he produces are absolutely earth shattering in terms of their dynamic volume. Little wonder the band just keep going, they are clearly enjoying themselves. This section alone makes *Welcome Back My Friends* an essential purchase!

'Tarkus' appears no less than fourteen times on the four box sets that make up the *Original Bootleg Series*. It is a virtual constant on all ELP's live albums, including their final *High Voltage* performance from 2016. Not surprising for such a demanding piece of music, cover versions have been few and far between. Some versions have appeared on ELP tribute albums – most notably 1999's *Encores, Legends & Paradox* album – as well as on *The Road Home*, an album by Dream Theater keyboard maestro, Jordan Rudess. Interestingly, on Rudess's cover, Steven Wilson – who remixed *Tarkus* for ELP for the 2012 deluxe edition – sang vocals on 'Stones of Years'. Keith Emerson, as a result of various solo projects and collaborations, released several live recordings of 'Tarkus'. These include *Live from California* (with Glenn Hughes and Marc Bonilla), *Three Fates Project* (an orchestral version conducted by Terje Mikkelsen and featuring Marc Bonilla) and *Live from Manticore Hall* (from 2010's live tour with Greg Lake).

## Side Two:

### 'Jeremy Bender' (Emerson, Lake)

The subject matter of the opening track from side two should probably be viewed with both a pinch of salt and the benefit of hindsight. 'Bender' is British slang for a homosexual male – a term widely used in the very un-PC early-1970s. One suggestion is that Lake's lyrics were attempting wordplay. In the USA, 'bender' means something completely different, commonly describing a drinking spree or a period of extended drug use. 'Going on a bender' is a phrase that wouldn't cause offence, even in the UK, so perhaps ELP were trying to be humorous? One can imagine the band on tour in the USA and hearing 'bender' spoken in the American context, laughing – rather immaturely it has to be said – at the difference between the two meanings.

Years later, Emerson wisely distanced himself from the lyrics and claimed, 'I didn't think about it, I was just happy to get some words up so I could play that honky tonk piano'. He says he was messing around with the chord progressions to the traditional American song, 'Oh! Susanna', playing it on a honky-tonk piano. 'After adding some fifth root chords to it, the band thought that was pretty cool. Then Greg came up with the words. It's sort of Floyd Kramer, the piano style – he was a great player. So it's me doing Floyd playing 'Oh! Susanna', if that makes any sense. We all thought it was a fun song. It lightened everything up.'

ELP's tendency to include humorous songs on their otherwise weightier progressive albums began with *Tarkus.* The first album was devoid of any light hearted moments, it was all earnest stuff. They had, of course, already been playing the novelty instrumental hit 'Nutrocker' as an encore number, as heard on *Pictures at an Exhibition.* Emerson also became renowned for including snippets of well known tunes during his improvised piano pieces, which in the British music hall tradition, always got laughter from the audience. The 'joke' tracks soon became part of ELP's appeal, showing they didn't take themselves too seriously. For a typical young male music fan in the seventies, tracks such as 'Jeremy Bender', 'The Sheriff' (from *Trilogy)* and "Benny the Bouncer" (from *Brain Salad Surgery*) all became an integral part of ELP's sound, whether on album or at gigs.

Admittedly, with regard to 'Jeremy Bender', what once may have caused titters of amusement among British schoolboys when the album was first released, now causes raised eyebrows – but there is no evidence ELP had an axe to grind against homosexuals. It is probably best to view 'Jeremy Bender' as the product of misguided humour. All said of course without wishing to defend the band in any way. It probably wasn't acceptable then and certainly isn't today.

In the band's live set, 'Jeremy Bender' was often paired with 'The Sheriff' and appears as such on the triple live LP, *Welcome Back My Friends.* On the *Original Bootleg Series* it appears just once. Very wisely, this curious track was not played live by the band after 1974.

## 'Bitches Crystal' (Emerson, Lake)

With a clear Dave Brubeck influence, 'Bitches Crystal' is a mutated boogie-woogie in 6/8. According to Emerson, 'We went in with a pretty strong idea, practised it to the point where we know what we were doing, and recorded it. The music is pretty hard in spots – we attacked it. Greg wasn't as keen on Brubeck as I was, but Carl was very taken with Dave's drummer, Joe Morello. You can hear that kind of feel here. Carl knew what he was up to.'

With a typical ELP twist, 'Bitches Crystal' begins with an almost music box (or is it an ice cream van?!) refrain. Played on a celesta – a small upright piano that sounds closer to a glockenspiel – it gently lures the listener into a false sense of security, only to be hit head-on by the full impact of the band playing the song's main theme. Lake's sci-fi lyrics help take the track into another dimension, a million miles away from Emerson's Brubeck influence. Not that the Moog overdubs leave you with any doubt that you're listening to prime-era ELP playing 1950s-tinged cool jazz! The Moog sounds impressively like French horns here, before Emerson begins a fast and furious piano solo as the track twists and turns, including a brief gentle return to the opening refrain. Lake puts in one of his best-ever 'rock' vocal performances – arguably surpassing his effected voice on King Crimson's '21st Century Schizoid Man'. At just under four minutes long, 'Bitches Crystal' is a perfect example ELP's ability to rock out. It is also an illustration of how lazy music journalists could be at the dawn of punk – yes, ELP played bombastic 20 minute epics, but they could also keep it short and to the point. Many have mourned that ELP didn't exploit this part of their multi-faceted personality more often.

It is somewhat of a surprise that 'Bitches Crystal' didn't find its way into ELP's live set during their 1970s heyday. It made a welcome late appearance in their set during the late-1990s – an excellent example is on the *Live in Poland* album. Carl Palmer obviously had a soft spot for the track as he played it live whilst in Qango and with his own trio. Sung by John Wetton, it features on Qango's only album,1997's *Live in the Hood*. The track also appears on *Working Live, Volume 3*, one of Palmer's three post-ELP live albums that pay homage to his former band. A cover of 'Bitches Crystal' was released by UK prog band Panic Room on their 2011 *Altitude* EP. As with Magenta's cover of 'Lucky Man', this was originally intended to appear on the cancelled Prog magazine ELP tribute CD.

## 'The Only Way / Hymn' (Emerson, Lake)
It has been questioned whether the next three tracks on *Tarkus* are conceptual, belonging not only together but also as part of the album's overall theme. Whether or not that was the band's intention, 'The Only Way' does have a lyrical direction roughly in line with side one. Although Lake was never forthcoming about the nature of his lyrics, Emerson later said, 'I have no idea about the words. I remember Greg going into the vocal booth to sing it. Carl and I were sitting in the control room wondering how it was all going to come out. Suddenly, we hear Greg sing, 'Why did he lose six million Jews?' That kind of halted the proceedings for a while. We had to consider that… thinking this is heavy.'

With Lake's lyrics to the fore and the classically-influenced music played by Emerson using the pipe organ at St Mark's Church, Finchley, 'The Only Way' is undisputedly an underrated gem. Emerson had discovered the organ at St Mark's, to the northwest of London, and became captivated by it. 'What a brilliant sound. I found this church organ and learned some Bach on it. It's a whole different approach playing a pipe organ, particularly when it comes to the feet – I'm not Fred Astaire on the foot pedals!' Built in 1878 by J.W. Walker, the organ was rebuilt in 1950 and in great condition when Emerson was recorded playing it using a mobile recording facility. 'There was no way to bring the pipe organ to Advision. And of course, in those days there were no computers to sample it. But it worked out well. I was quite pleased. Greg and I realised that we had a song and he went off to work out the lyrics'.

The second half of the track sees the pipe organ give way to jazzy piano, bass and drums, Lake's words ramming home his point that 'Man is man-made'. Free of Moog overdubs and any bombastic treatment, 'The Only Way' was mixed with space to breathe, Eddie Offord's engineering and Lake's production deserving special credit. Working admirably with the 16 tracks available to them at Advision, Lake's double-tracked vocal refrains are the only obvious evidence of overdubbing.

### 'Infinite Space (Conclusion)' (Emerson, Palmer)
Seamlessly running straight from 'The Only Way', this piano led piece – played on a seven foot Bechstein – is Emerson's attempt at a more laidback vibe after the 'heavy' lyrics of the previous track. 'It's a good time signature. It wasn't me trying to be clever, it just seemed to work. I thought there could have been a vocal over it, even if it was a bit 'Rio De Janeiro' in feel. World music was in the back of my mind'. Emerson's words give doubt that there was any particular concept at play here, although the piece has been analysed as the musical equivalent of 'life going on', the repeating piano figure representing mankind's returning again and again to the same paths. Lake's contribution is restricted to low key bass guitar. Palmer, however, gets a credit – a rarity on *Tarkus* – Emerson praising the drummer's contribution, saying that he made several great suggestions, encouraging him to play on the off beat with his right hand.

### 'A Time and a Place' (Emerson, Lake, Palmer)
Along with the album's closing track, 'A Time and a Place' is a full band composition. Emerson, rather surprisingly, claims that he was influenced by Led Zeppelin when writing the song. 'ELP and Zeppelin rehearsed in the same area back then. I know I was listening to a lot of Zeppelin. Black Dog was a really good one. Jimmy Page was a mate of mine'.

Emerson said that they did around three takes of 'A Time and a Place', although, apart from the original, none surfaced on 2012's deluxe edition, more's the shame. 'I play a lot of unison lines in the song, and they work out well and create a lot of power. The recording went very smoothly. Once we'd got the 'Tarkus' epic on side one done, everything else was fairly easy. There's some good keyboard sounds on here. I was sticking with the Moog and the Hammond B3. I never mentioned being influenced by Zeppelin to Jimmy Page – when you meet up with people socially, you never get into that stuff at all!' Listening now, the track certainly has a heavy rock vibe, Emerson's glorious distorted Hammond riffs pushing Lake's vocals hard – which sound strained at times. One wonders how 'A Time and a Place' would have sounded with Bonham-style drumming as Palmer seems to struggle to play the kind of groove that could have elevated the track into classic rock territory.

### 'Are You Ready Eddy?' (Emerson, Lake, Palmer)
The final track on *Tarkus* can either be seen as a filler, or as a fun tribute to their studio engineer, Eddie Offord. 'Are you ready Eddy?' was the band's

catchphrase during the recording of the album. Emerson remembers, 'We were having what you'd call a wrap party to celebrate finishing the record. Greg, Carl and myself grew out of that time of rock'n'roll, letting your hair down music. We were a fun band... we definitely had a sense of humour'.

Serious music critics have frequently condemned this rollicking finale. Some progressive music experts, critiquing *Tarkus*, even ignore it completely. What these po-faced critics forget is that 'Are You Ready Eddy?' is the sound of ELP showing another side to their musical personalities. Is it progressive rock? No. But it is nonetheless a vital part of what made ELP the band they were – and it certainly showed they could play four-to-the-floor and get feet tapping. And lest we forget, this short, two minute blast of Jerry Lee Lewis style rock'n'roll, was recorded in just a single take. It isn't meant to be perfect and it isn't meant to be clever – there are plenty of other ELP tracks that fulfil that need.

The band's banter at the end of this track has always been a mystery to non-British fans. By way of an explanation, what they are actually shouting, in their best Dick Van Dyke 'Mockney' accents, is a light-hearted reference to the lady at Advision's canteen who, when asked what sandwiches she had, would always reply, 'ham or cheese'!

## *Tarkus* rarities and bonus tracks

2012 Steven Wilson BMG deluxe edition
Serial numbers: Sony/Legacy/Manticore 88691937962 (UK & Europe release), Razor & Tie 7930183348-2 (USA & Canada)
Released in September 2012 as a double CD and DVDA set, this is by far the most definitive issue of *Tarkus* to-date. Although remixed by Steven Wilson, relatively few bonus tracks are included. It is nonetheless a fascinating record of the band's recording sessions at that time. The first CD is a remastered original album, whereas the second is the 'alternative *Tarkus*'. This features new stereo mixes by Wilson, plus 'Oh, My Father', 'Unknown Ballad' and a different, instrumental take of 'Mass'.

'Oh, My Father' is a Greg Lake song recorded during the Tarkus sessions but left off the album. The song was written by Lake after the death of his Father. 'Unknown Ballad' is the source of quite a bit of controversy. To be blunt, it sounds nothing like ELP – including the vocals. Much was posted online about this song after its inclusion, fans guessing who was singing – Emerson being the common assumption. The truth is that this is an outtake from an adhoc session by the band Spontaneous Combustion. According to the band's bass player, Tristram Margetts, Greg had invited them to Advision Studios, where ELP were recording *Tarkus*. Keith and Carl had to leave early, so Greg had the idea of recording what turned out to be 'Unknown Ballad'. 'There was no prior knowledge or arrangement, it was literally spontaneous! The singer is my brother Gary Margetts. I put down a simple bass track and I think Greg played piano and we all sang backing vocals – including Tony Brock our drummer.

When we were waiting in the control room, Eddie Offord told us he had just finished the final mix of an up and coming band, would we like to hear it? It was *The Yes Album*! Quite some experience for a 15 year old kid!' Singer Gary Margetts also confirmed the story, saying that, 'It was the first song I'd ever written'.

Spontaneous Combustion were from Poole in Dorset, close to where Lake was born and brought up. They initially called themselves Transit Sound but at Lake's suggestion they re-named themselves Spontaneous Combustion. With his help, they gained a record deal with Harvest, and Lake produced their debut album. They famously supported ELP on the night *Pictures at an Exhibition* was recorded.

The track's inclusion as part of the *Tarkus* deluxe set was obviously in error, although it is something Wilson has refused to be drawn on. Whether its presence is down to him or not, what remains a mystery is why anyone ever thought it was ELP in the first place?

2012 Steven Wilson double CD BMG issue
Serial number: BMGCAT2CD2
This two CD set includes the original remastered album plus Steven Wilson's 2012 stereo mixes (but not the 5.1 surround sound mixes), as well as the bonus tracks, including 'Unknown Ballad'. Despite rumours this errant track would be deleted after its source had been correctly identified, it never has been.

2014 Steven Wilson double vinyl edition
Serial number: MOVLP591
A double vinyl album issue that includes the original remastered album plus Steven Wilson's 2012 'alternative *Tarkus*' stereo mixes, but only including 'Mass' as a bonus track.

2014 Victory Japanese limited edition
Serial number: VICP-78002
A limited edition, remastered Japanese edition 'Platinum SHM-CD' presented in a cardboard mini replica sleeve. The interesting thing about this issue is the bonus track, 'Prelude And Fugue' – which had originally appeared on the band's Return of the Manticore box set in 1993. Incorrectly attributed to the entire band, this is in fact an Emerson piano-etude, composed by the Austrian composer and pianist, Friedrich Gulda.

# Pictures at an Exhibition (1971)

Personnel:
Keith Emerson: Hammond organ, piano, Moog synthesiser IC
Greg Lake: vocals, bass, acoustic guitar, electric guitar
Carl Palmer: drums & percussion
Released: November 1971 (UK), January 1972 (USA)
Recorded: Newcastle City Hall, 26 March, 1971
Hight chart places: 2 in UK, 10 US Billboard 200.

Although recorded at Newcastle City Hall on ELP's second tour, on 26 March 1971, *Pictures at an Exhibition* had been in ELP's set since their inception. Written by the Russian composer Modeste Petrovich Mussorgsky, it was best known as an orchestrated piece, as arranged by Ravel. That is how Keith Emerson first heard it, performed at The Royal Festival Hall in London. Still in The Nice at the time, he bought the score the following day and was pleasantly surprised to discover it was originally intended as a piano piece. The idea to arrange it must have stayed in his mind, as when ELP were formed he proposed the idea to Greg Lake and Carl Palmer. They agreed and set about working on it at their early rehearsals in London during the Summer of 1970.

Mussorgsky's suite describes the composer's experience when viewing the posthumous 1874 art exhibition of his friend and artist, Viktor Hartman. The score was apparently completed in twenty days and features just ten of over 400 paintings at the exhibition. Mussorgsky linked his musical descriptions of these ten paintings with five 'promenades' – passages which reflected his changing mood as he mused on his friend's life – affected by the paintings he had just seen, or in anticipation of another work glimpsed as he walked toward it.

ELP's adaptation fused the original classical score with an eclectic and exciting mix of rock, blues, jazz and folk – in a mode that echoes the earlier work of both The Nice and King Crimson. The band adapted only two paintings from Mussorgsky's work, linking them with three 'promenades' plus additional self-composed pictures and improvisations of their own. Their arrangement was first aired to a small audience of record company executives and the band's roadies, on 21 August 1970, at the Lyceum Theatre in London. A couple of days later, at ELP's very first gig – a warm up for the Isle of Wight Festival at the Guildhall in Plymouth – *Pictures* was the centrepiece of their set. It would remain an integral part of their live performance until 1998.

By the time ELP reached Newcastle, on their second tour, on 26 March 1971, *Pictures* was a staple of their set. The band had become a well oiled machine and were playing with supreme confidence to enthusiastic audiences. Crucially, on the mixing desk that night, was Eddie Offord. His familiarity with the band's sound already honed thanks to his engineering duties during the recording sessions for *Tarkus* in late 1970. Offord not only captured the performance of a band in their prime, he created an excellent quality recording. This was in direct contrast to the band's previous attempt at recording *Pictures at an*

*Exhibition* on 9 December 1970, just days after returning from a series of European dates. The show, at London's Lyceum Theatre, was specially put on to capture their performance on film. However, the band were not happy with either their playing, or the quality of the filming that night. Worse, when Greg Lake was given the 8-track master tapes, he was appalled to discover spillage across the tracks. This made creating a successful mix, to the quality expected of a band like ELP, a near impossibility. Lake refused to sanction its release as a soundtrack although the film, much to the band's disapproval, was given a limited cinema release.

Disappointed, ELP pledged to record another gig at a later date. It is unclear why the Newcastle City Hall gig was chosen – possibly because of the Hall's excellent acoustics and its reputation for a positive audience reaction, but maybe also because of the Hall's famed Harrison and Harrison pipe organ. Emerson's penchant for playing pipe organs had already manifested itself on ELP's debut album (using the Royal Festival Hall's organ on 'Clotho' from 'The Three Fates') and on *Tarkus* (using the organ at St Mark's, Finchley, on 'The Only Way'). Using the Newcastle City Hall pipe organ at the City Hall was possibly an opportunity too good to miss.

ELP's performance from that night in Newcastle is magnificent – resulting in arguably the band's finest live recording, eclipsing all other ELP versions of *Pictures* before or since. Although the band were justifiably pleased with the results, ELP's record company had to decide what to do with it. With *Tarkus* still unreleased at this point, a double album with *Pictures* was briefly considered. Greg Lake was quoted in the music press as saying, 'We are thinking of including it but making no extra charge'. In the end, that plan was shelved, presumably for cost reasons, and *Tarkus* was released on its own. *Pictures*, for a while, was left in the can and eventually released in the UK in November 1971 – at the budget price of £1.49.

It reached number three in the UK album charts but plans to issue the album in America stalled. ELP's US label, Atlantic, worried about its appeal to a non-European audience. They suggested, instead, that it could be issued on an Atlantic subsidiary label, Nonsuch. ELP strongly voiced their objections, perplexed that *Pictures* wasn't being seen as a bona fide ELP release. The situation was eventually resolved when import copies of *Pictures* began to get airplay on US FM radio, often in its 40 minute entirety. As import sales soared – reportedly selling as many as 50,000 copies – Atlantic relented, eventually releasing the album in January 1972. It went on to reach number 10 in the USA charts, staying in the top 40 for three months.

*Pictures* became a cornerstone release for both ELP and progressive rock in general. Hi-fi retailers used the album to demonstrate their latest stereo systems, and music teachers played it to pupils in an attempt to inspire and educate them in classical music. Fittingly, the latter was one of Emerson's original intentions, hoping to pass on his passion for classical composition to rock music fans. Although pilloried by rock music critics for this approach, it is an aim he achieved. In the wake of ELP's *Pictures at an Exhibition*, classical labels reported a healthy upsurge in the music of Mussorgsky!

Despite initially charting highly in the UK, a change of rules at the beginning of 1972 excluded budget albums – resulting in ELP's *Pictures at an Exhibition* disappearing after a run of only five weeks. Its last chart position before being disallowed was number nine.

## 'Promenade' (Mussorgsky)

Keith Emerson's immortal words, 'We're gonna give you *Pictures at an Exhibition*', announced the band's performance at Newcastle City Hall – words that have ever since been linked with ELP's playing of Mussorgsky's famous work. Thereafter, *Pictures* was always announced in the same way – up to and including their final concert at London's High Voltage Festival on 25 July, 2010.

With the passionate Geordie audience roaring its approval, Emerson, sitting high above the stage in front of the City Hall's famed Harrison & Harrison pipe organ, began playing the album's first track, 'Promenade'. The organ, with its impressive 4,274 pipes, was installed when the hall was first built in 1928. Described as a 'Rolls-Royce' among pipe organs, it is still in pride of place today. One can imagine Keith Emerson being irresistibly drawn to it on that night in 1971, his playing a fitting testament to the original composition and the historic instrument's impressive dynamics.

The first of three 'promenades' in ELP's interpretation of *Pictures*, the opening track is arguably the closest to Mussorgsky's original. Free of the rock, jazz and blues influences that mark other pieces on the album, it is nonetheless a powerful musical statement. The range and versatility of the organ in Emerson's hands gives the track a fanfare-like quality, full of the pomp and majesty that became an ELP hallmark.

Although written by Mussorgsky to represent walking between paintings at the exhibition, ELP chose to also represent 'Promenade' as a work hung on the wall of the wooden-panelled gallery depicted on the album sleeve. Presented as what looks like a blank canvas, presented in a plain white frame, it is in fact a white dove painted on a white background – the image too subtle to been seen in print. Artist William Neal said that the dove was his homage to Nic Dartnell's cover design for ELP's debut album.

## 'The Gnome' (Mussorgsky / Palmer)

As the massive sound of the pipe organ fades, Carl Palmer's drum rolls act as an interlude, giving Emerson just enough time to get back down to the stage for all three musicians to unite to play 'The Gnome'. It is one of only three of the original Mussorgsky paintings represented in ELP's version of *Pictures*. With Emerson behind his Hammond and Greg Lake playing a Fender Jazz Bass through a wah-wah pedal, Palmer's confident drumming takes the lead – fully warranting his joint composer credit on the track. He guides the trio through a series of fractured stops and starts in an assured adaptation of the composition, instantly recognisable to anyone familiar with either Ravel's classical arrangement or Mussorgsky's solo piano original.

At around the minute mark, Emerson's growling Hammond gloriously underpins Lake's distorted bass before the keyboard maestro unleashes the sound of his modular Moog synthesiser. Resplendent in one of his striking stage outfits, playing the synth with one hand and the Hammond with the other, Emerson was every inch a 1970s keyboard 'wizard'. Although his astonishing keyboard technique and flamboyant showmanship became the focus of every ELP live performance, it would be a huge mistake to ignore the contributions of Lake and Palmer on this track as their playing is as accomplished as anything the keyboardist conjures up. And as future band forays and experiments would later evidence, both were totally irreplaceable. 'The Gnome' clearly demonstrates that ELP were a sum of their parts.

In the art exhibition of 1874 that had inspired Mussorgsky to write *Pictures at an Exhibition*, the artist Viktor Hartmann's 'Gnomus' – retitled 'The Gnome' by ELP – was a design for a giant nutcracker, depicted with menacing teeth. Mussorgsky's composition, with its frequent tempo changes, suggested the grotesque creature lurching as it walked. Emerson's creative use of the Moog captures this ungainly gait with a series of siren-like swoops, before he generates a wall of synthesised white noise. Faithful to the original piece in spirit, if not instrumentation, one hopes Mussorgsky would approve of ELP's bold treatment as Emerson gets back behind his Hammond for a rousing finale – surprisingly uplifting rather than a dark musical description of evil intent.

'The Gnome' in ELP's gallery, as depicted on the inside of the gatefold sleeve, was also painted by William Neil. Neil was responsible for not only creating the painting but for the design of the sleeve itself. His painting here shows just the eyes and nose of the gnome, its baleful eyes at odds with the sharpened teeth of Hartmann's design. It seems without menace – more a creature to pity than fear.

## 'Promenade' (Mussorgsky / Lake)

Eschewing the Harrison & Harrison pipe organ for one of his two Hammond organs, Emerson sensitively revisits the 'Promenade' theme in tandem with Lake's vocals. Singing initially acapella, Lake stays close to the main melody, singing three verses of self-penned lyrics. In the original work, each time the 'Promenade' theme is played, it evokes a different emotion. The first is full of grandeur – a proud announcement of the exhibition, bursting with importance. The second, as here, is more restrained, describing the emotions of Mussorgsky as he viewed the exhibition, reflecting on the painting he had just seen. There is also anticipation, of the next painting, glimpsed just ahead.

## 'The Sage' (Lake)

In Mussorgsky's original work, the second painting was 'The Old Castle'. In ELP's version, it is a painting of their own, a Greg Lake composition entitled 'The Sage'. It is of great credit to ELP they didn't simply copy and adapt

*Pictures at an Exhibition* in their own style. Instead, they introduced new elements, 'The Sage' opening with restrained Hammond from Emerson, punctuated by his flamboyant Moog. As the Moog fades, Lake's arpeggiated acoustic guitar chords and rich vocals take centre stage. The vocal melody bears a resemblance to Grieg's 'Solveig's Song' from *Peer Gynt* but is nonetheless a beautiful ballad in its own right.

To anyone hearing *Pictures at an Exhibition* for the first time by listening to the ELP version – which was probably the vast majority of rock fans –'The Sage' is a perfect fit. Stylistically, it gives the album a widespread progressive feel that listeners familiar with King Crimson would feel comfortable with. Sung and played by Lake on his favoured Gibson J-200 guitar, 'The Sage' is one of his most underrated acoustic compositions, notable for some technically adept guitar playing – especially in the song's sophisticated instrumental middle section. With his guitar somewhat impersonating the tone of a lute, Lake's accomplished playing has an Elizabethan feel – evidence perhaps of his guitar lessons as a boy. As he adeptly switches from using a pick to fingers during the instrumental action, showing that his guitar lessons were well spent. It is interesting to note that although Greg Lake shared the same teacher with King Crimson's Robert Fripp from their school days together in Dorset, the styles of the two guitarists could not be more different. It has long been said that Lake doesn't get the credit he deserves for his guitar playing – 'The Sage' amply affirms this.

The track's inclusion as part of ELP's *Pictures at an Exhibition* emphasises that the band weren't just trying to adapt Mussorsky's work for an electronic rock band, they were instead using the composition as a foundation and springboard to create something new and exciting. By including new music such as this, they helped sweeten the original piece for a new rock audience; an aim in which they succeeded admirably.

William's Neil's painting for 'The Sage' adds an added air of mystery. In muted tones, the face of a wizened old man can be discerned, hidden among the mass of vigorous tangles of writhing shapes. Are these shapes the sage's hair or are they his thoughts and emotions? In fact, according to Neil, it is a abstract impression of Lake's dogs, two red setters! These dogs can be seen at Lake's side in the *Manticore Special* documentary on the band.

## 'The Old Castle' (Mussorgsky / Emerson)

As the last guitar chord of 'The Sage' fades and the audience warmly applauds, Emerson whips out his ribbon controller. Connected to the Moog by a long length of cable, this touch sensitive strip allowed Emerson to control the pitch of his synthesiser by running his fingers along its length. Ever the showman, Emerson brandished the ribbon controller in a phallus-like manner, his suggestive hand movements along the controller's length allowing the keyboard star to engage in theatrics not dissimilar to that of Hendrix some years earlier. It also gave him the chance to step away from his huge bank of keyboards, allowing him wander to the edge of the stage, and at times into the audience.

With Emerson and his ribbon controller unleashing screams of raw synthesised sound at the beginning of 'The Old Castle', accompanied by Palmer's impressive freeform drumming, the audience responded enthusiastically. Only by viewing old film footage of the band can you understand why! Theatrics and showmanship were an important part of ELP's performance during their early years, Emerson gaining a well-won reputation as the 'Hendrix' of keyboards players, abusing his Hammond organ as he threw it around the stage and squeezing unholy sounds from his Moogs. As he duels with Palmer during 'The Old Castle' – in a classic call and response manner – Emerson finally hits a thunderously low note on his synth, which is the cue for the track to kick into life. With Lake and Palmer locking in with an infectious backbeat, they provide a solid platform for an extended synth solo, Emerson making full use of the monophonic Moog's sweeping portamento.

To many of those listening to the album who hadn't seen ELP live – the author included – the source of the sounds here were a mystery. This of course simply added to the growing mystique that surrounded ELP and their banks of equipment. Talk at the time was very much of Emerson and his huge 'telephone exchange' Moog, Palmer's accomplished lengthy drum solos and the futuristic sci-fi landscapes conjured up by Lake's sonorous vocals. ELP were the undisputed kings in a 'Top Trumps' of progressive rock heroes – faster, bigger and better. The approach was largely encouraged by the band themselves as they pushed themselves to ever greater heights in terms of musicality and presentation.

Borrowing snatches of melody from the Mussorgsky original, ELP treat 'The Old Castle' as an uptempo jam – in direct contrast to the classical piece's original pastoral feel. Critics have blasted ELP for the treatment, claiming the band's bombastic playing ignores the reverent and considered description of Hartmann's painting. Without question, ELP's playing here is the very epitome of a 'rocked up classic', in a style broadly despised by the band's detractors. Yet, for their fans, the track is a glorious example of the band cutting loose and improvising. Emerson's Moog sounds fabulously strident, with Palmer's insistent snare drum driving the track relentlessly forward.

But did the critics have a point? Maybe, as one does wonder how 'The Old Castle' would have sounded if treated with restraint, perhaps in the same vein as 'Take a Pebble'. It certainly would have more accurately reflected Hartmann's painting, which was rather delicately executed in the style of an old Italian watercolour. Created on a trip to France, the tower in the background of Hartmann's work bears a strong resemblance to the Catholic cathedral in Périgueux, in the Dordogne region of France. In response to ELP's more aggressive playing, William Neil chose to paint a fantasy castle instead. This was later revived for the cover of Carl Palmer's *Working Live - Volume 3*', an album of live interpretations of ELP classics – including *Pictures at an Exhibition*. Today, the painting hangs proudly in the drummer's home.

### 'Blues Variation' (Emerson / Lake / Palmer)

With 'The Old Castle' reaching a climax, Emerson fired up his Hammond and led the band through the groove-laden 'Blues Variation'. Running seamlessly from the previous track – marked from the moment the Moog ceases and the 1960s-style organ-driven romp begins – 'Blues Variation' allows Emerson to play some seriously soulful Hammond, with a sizeable nod to the legendary Bill Evans 1963 classic 'Interplay'. As with 'The Sage', this is a new ELP 'painting'. It is the glorious sound of the trio playing as a unit, stripped back to Hammond, bass and drums. Carefree and full of exuberance, 'Blues Variation' typifies ELP's core sound in way they failed to maximise on during their latter years. It is also as close to the style of The Nice that ELP ever got, and a welcome reminder that, at heart, ELP were a rock band that could get heads in the front row enthusiastically nodding in appreciation. 'Blues Variation' was a fine way to round off side one of the original vinyl album.

### 'Promenade' (Mussorgsky)

With Palmer playing a tight military drum roll on his snare, Emerson's Moog emits a barrage of laser sharp sequences – all very lo-fi 70s sci-fi – before he re-introduces the 'Promenade' theme on his Hammond. This third and final 'Promenade' on ELP's *Pictures at an Exhibition* is a close repeat but a different arrangement of the album's opening track.

Mussorgsky's third 'Promenade' is a similar but different composition. In many ways, it is a shame ELP chose not to interpret the other Mussorgsky versions of 'Promenade' – the fourth, in particular, would have made an excellent laidback counterpoint to some of the band's musical excesses. Then again, excess and bombast is very much what ELP were about, that 'Marmite' quality that made them such a 'love 'em or hate 'em' band! Here, with bass and drums powerfully backing Emerson, it is very much a rock treatment, aggressive and full of pomp. Lake's bass is interesting in that it follows the left hand of the original piano score – thus acting as an effective balance to Emerson's overdriven Hammond, which in itself is stylistically similar to his playing on the band's first album.

### 'The Hut of Baba Yaga Part One' (Mussorgsky)

Originally called The Hut on Fowl's Legs, ELP renamed it 'The Hut Of Baba Yaga'. The track tells the story of Baba Yaga, a witch from Russian folklore. In the tale, whenever Baba Yaga hears someone approaching, her hut – which was perched on chicken's feet – turns to face them. The unsuspecting guests are lured inside to face an untimely end, Baba Yaga rather grimly grinding her victim's bones using a pestle and mortar before eating them. Somewhat bizarrely, the mortar, when not being used for such a grisly purpose, flies the witch through the sky. It is this flight that Mussorgsky describes, his music seething with malevolence.

ELP's version sees Lake's bass playing lock horns with Emerson's Hammond as Palmer's snare drum introduces a naggingly persistent beat. Playing in unison, they create a furiously powerful riff – an effective roughly hewn representation of Mussorgsky's original score. Emerson's gritty Hammond sounds glorious in this short sharp shock of a track, lasting just 1:28 minutes. Who said that all prog rock tracks were over-long?

We can assume that Mussorgsky's music was inspired by the folktales rather than Hartmann's work at the exhibition, which in this case was an overly decorative design for a clock in the shape of Baba Yaga's hut. For the ELP sleeve, William Neil chose to depict a image of a much simpler hut – more akin to a dovecot sitting atop a tall pole. Eagle-eyed fans will notice that the background stripes in the painting bear a strong resemblance to those on the *Tarkus* album cover.

## 'The Curse of Baba Yaga' (Emerson / Lake / Palmer)

Opening with distorted wah-wah bass played over a shimmering Hammond, this ELP composition introduces another new painting to the exhibition. The track kicks into life at just under the minute mark, when Lake plays a jazz-tinged bass riff in E to introduce an upfront drum pattern from Palmer – complete with Moog histrionics from Emerson. Fuzz bass, aggressive Hammond and ferocious drumming pushes the playing ever harder, Lake's half-shouted vocals adding to the urgency. The track ends with a slightly detuned Moog solo over frantic bass and drums, the band seemingly teetering at the edge of control.

Arguably the best of the paintings created for ELP by William Neil, this aggressive track is represented by a large, menacing, black disc in a violent sky, above what looks to be a rampaging hoard of demonic alien-like creatures, their red mouths open with evil intent. This sci-fi image – again with echoes of *Tarkus* – perfectly matches ELP's sinister composition. Like all the paintings on the inside of the gatefold, it makes one wish it had been reproduced larger, to help gain fuller appreciation of Neil's atmospheric work.

## 'The Hut of Baba Yaga Part Two' (Mussorgsky)

As the tempo increases ever further, the heavy-hitting main 'Baba Yaga' riff is revised, seamlessly running from the previous track. With all three musicians playing in tight unison, the interplay between Emerson's Hammond and Palmer's energetic drumming is nothing short of astonishing – underpinned by Lake's angry bass. The band's youthful level of energy is fantastic to hear – testament to the quality of Eddie Offord's audio engineering and ELP's fearless 'anything goes' attitude at this point in their career. Again, this is a short track – a shade over a minute long – the band showing admirable restraint as they play as a unit rather than giving in to the kind of self indulgent soloing that marked many other progressive rock tracks of the era.

## 'The Great Gates of Kiev' (Mussorgsky, Lake)

*The Great Gates of Kiev* – originally titled *The Bogatyr Gates* (In the Capital in Kiev) – was the final piece in both Mussorgsky's *Pictures at an Exhibition* and ELP's version. Mussorgsky's uplifting score is his finest and most recognisable work. Full of grandeur, the music describes a triumphant religious procession in celebration of Tsar Alexander II. Hartmann's design at the original exhibition was for a monumental gate to the Tsar following the monarch's narrow escape from an assassination attempt in 1866.

The design – which Hartmann was exceedingly proud of – was created in response to an architectural competition, commissioned by the Tsar for a new city gate. For unknown reasons, plans to build the gate were later shelved. Rather confusingly, two ancient gates in Kiev actually do exist – the Golden Gates of Kiev, which date from the 11th century, and the city's Southern Gate, which is sometimes known as the Great Gate of Kiev. Neither have any connection with Mussorgsky's composition or Hartmann.

ELP's version closely follows Mussorgsky's original but with the addition of lyrics and vocals. Lake's choirboy-style singing adds a strange unsettling dimension, giving colour and the illusion of meaning, his obtuse lyrics being somewhat open to interpretation. He seems to sing about an oppressed people being drawn through the gates, to be delivered into a new life or to their deaths. This is in direct contrast to Mussorgsky's musical description of a religious procession passing through the gates in a reverent celebration of Tsar Alexander II's life. Lake's closing phrase 'There's no end to my life, no beginning to my death, death is life' is nonetheless a fine finale, triumphantly closing both the album and the exhibition.

Neil's painting of the track depicts an acute view of two huge metallic gates – futuristic and other-worldly. Instead of thinking of ancient Russian heroes or tsars, we imagine post-apocalyptic worlds and civilisations. Are those oppressed people we can see gathering inside the gates? Lake's lyrics 'dark hidden seams, where the fossil sun gleams' is something that Neil surely picked up on evidenced by the dark red 'fossil sun' gleaming dimly in the alien sky. Perhaps it is an imagining of a civilisation coming to an end? What is certain is that the combination of ELP's music and Neil's artwork pours new light on Mussorgsky's original *Pictures at an Exhibition*, opening it up to a new audience. Together, they are both powerful and compelling.

## 'Nutrocker' (Tchaikovsky, Fowley, arranged by Emerson, Lake, Palmer)

Perhaps because the shorter length of side two, ELP decided to include 'Nutrocker', one of their two encore numbers at the time. Originally an instrumental hit for B. Bumble and the Stingers in May 1962 – reaching number one in the UK charts and number 23 in the Billboard Hot 100 in the USA – it is based on Tchailovsky's 'March of the Toy Soldiers' from his *Nutcracker* ballet suite. It has occasionally been said that Greg Lake wasn't very keen on playing the track, claiming it was too gimmicky. Apparently, he also wasn't enamoured with playing 'Rondo', the band's other encore number – mainly because of its link to Emerson's past with The Nice. One wonders what his choice of encore number would have been?

For the ELP version, 'Nut Rocker' was spelled as one word, 'Nutrocker'. Emerson plays the track using his five octave Hohner Clavinet – the same keyboard used for 'Tank' on ELP's first album. Its use on *Pictures* marks its final appearance on an ELP album. 'Nutrocker' continued to be played live until the band's 1977-78 tour, when Emerson played it on a Yamaha CP-70 electric piano.

The track was surprisingly released as an ELP single in the USA, Japan, Argentina and Mexico. It reached number 70 on the US Billboard Hot 100 and number 92 on Cashbox. The b-side was 'The Great Gates of Kiev'. In 2009, Trans-Siberian Orchestra released their own version, featuring Greg Lake. It appears on their album *Night Castle*.

ELP played 'Nutrocker' on *Pictures at an Exhibition* at a blistering pace, lacing it with self-depreciating humour – an approach they don't get enough credit for. Despite being serious progressive rock musicians, they were far from the po-faced 'dinosaurs' that punk widely derided them as, displaying both humour and a willingness to entertain. The energy and enthusiasm displayed on 'Nutrocker' can clearly be heard and by the time this gig was recorded one can only assume Lake's reluctance to play it had long since evaporated!

## *Pictures at an Exhibition* rarities and bonus tracks

1999 D2 Vision CD/DVD
Serial number: DVP001
A two disc CD / DVD release that has the original album on the CD plus the 9 December 1970 Lyceum gig on the DVD. The latter is the performance that received a limited released in cinemas across the UK in February 1971 (in a triple bill somewhat bizarrely also featuring films of The Strawbs and Scaffold). The footage infamously includes psychedelic film effects and cartoon graphics, something that most ELP fans think detracts from the performance. Sadly, the original unadulterated concert footage is believed to have been lost.

2001 Castle Music remastered edition
Serial number: CMRCD167
The is the remastered original album plus the 1993 studio version of *Pictures at an Exhibition* originally included as part of *The Return of the Manticore* box set.

2004 Sanctuary Midline
Serial number: SMRCD057
The has the original album plus the 1993 studio version originally included in *The Return of the Manticore* box set. The insert is a unique and informative 12-page fold-out booklet – well worth having!

2008 Sanctuary deluxe edition
Serial number: 1776980
The original remastered album, from 1993's *Return of the Manticore*, plus
audio of the 9 December 1970 Lyceum gig. The latter includes 'Pictures at an
Exhibition' as well as 'The Barbarian', 'Knife Edge', Rondo and 'Nutrocker'.

2016 BMG deluxe edition
Serial number: BMGCAT2CD3
As well as the original remastered album, this double CD set has audio of the 9
December 1970 Lyceum gig – 'Pictures at an Exhibition', 'The Barbarian', 'Knife
Edge',' Rondo' and 'Nutrocker' – plus the band's performance of *Pictures at
an Exhibition* at the Mar Y Sol Festival in Puerto Rico on 4th December 1972.
The 16-track master of the raw and exciting cut down version of *Pictures at
an Exhibition* from the Mar Y Sol Festival was rediscovered in 2006. It was
originally released in 2007, included as part of the *From the Beginning* box set,
and subsequently appeared, with the rest of the band's set from the festival, as
*Live at the Mar Y Sol Festival '72* in 2011. A various artists double live LP of the
festival, entitled *Mar Y Sol,* was issued in 1972, but ELP were only represented
by 'Take A Pebble' and 'Lucky Man'.

# Trilogy (1972)

Personnel:

Keith Emerson: Hammond organ C3, Steinway piano, zoukra, Moog synthesiser III C, Mini Moog model D

Greg Lake: vocals, bass, electric & acoustic Guitars

Carl Palmer: drums & Percussion

Released: 6 July 1972 (simultaneously in UK and USA)

Recorded: Advision Studios, London, late 1971 and early 1972

Highest chart place: 2 UK, 5 US Billboard 200

For ELP's fourth release in just two years, the band returned to London's Advision Studios buoyed by their increasing popularity. With Greg Lake once more in the producer's chair and Eddie Offord again on engineering duties, *Trilogy* saw ELP tackle a broader musical landscape. Ambitious and wide-ranging, it is the sound of the band at their peak – a sentiment echoed by Greg Lake, who frequently stated that *Trilogy* was his favourite ELP album. The recording sessions began before the band undertook a short US tour at the end of 1971, Keith Emerson announcing to the audience at their 12 November gig at The Music Hall in Boston that they'd recently been in the studio. Indeed, their opening number that night was the as-yet-unreleased 'Hoedown'. Snippets of both 'The Fugue' and 'The Sheriff' also made an appearance that night during Keith's piano improvisations in 'Take a Pebble'. 'Hoedown' was still opening the set by the time they played Madison Square Garden on 25 November – the last date of the tour – after which they flew back to the UK to complete the album.

More accessible to a non-hardcore progressive rock audience than *Tarkus*, *Trilogy*'s polished songwriting and state-of-the-art studio production saw the album rise to number two in the UK album charts, peaking at number five on the US Billboard 200. Arguably, if one had to choose a single album to introduce ELP to the casual listener, *Trilogy* would be the one. Critical reception was mostly positive, although *Trilogy* did gain one notorious write-up from the American music journalist Robert Christgau. After hearing the new album for a Billboard magazine review, he proclaimed that, 'These guys are as stupid as their most pretentious fans. Really, anybody who buys a record that divides a composition called 'The Endless Enigma' into two discrete parts deserves it.' Christgau, who labelled himself as an 'opinionated bigmouth', was renowned for playing to the gallery to illicit outrage, so perhaps his comments should be taken with a pinch of salt. Nevertheless, for any band who had worked hard to write and record a new album, such comments would have been irritating in the extreme.

Listening to *Trilogy* today, it is clear that the band's growing confidence in studio led to a layering of instrumentation that wasn't present on previous albums. Add to this the ever-growing arsenal of musical instruments at their disposal – most notably, Emerson's new Mini Moog – and the result is a far more sophisticated band sound with a wider tonal palate. This eventually led to a problems with playing the songs live, although to their credit during their 1972 tours, they did attempt 'The Endless Enigma', 'The Sheriff', 'Trilogy', and the album's epic closer, 'Abaddon's Bolero'. 'Hoedown' was already in the set before *Trilogy* was released, becoming their opening number for many years. It remained in the set until their final gig. Surprisingly it wasn't until their reunion in the early-90s that the big hit single off the album, 'From the Beginning', was played in its entirety.

Initially released on Island in the UK and Cotillon in the USA, *Trilogy* was given a gatefold cover, designed by Hipgnosis. William Neal, who designed and painted the covers for both *Tarkus* and *Pictures at an Exhibition*, was originally briefed to create the artwork. However, his ideas weren't chosen by the band. 'My work with ELP came to a close while working on *Trilogy*. It was not a conceptual album, more a reaching out into more personal images of photographs and portraits. In hindsight, my contribution of ideas was at 'burn-out' on many levels – although I did submit an interesting image for the track 'The Endless Enigma' as a cover idea. This remains a silent legacy as to what might have been!'

Once Neil and ELP parted company, Hipgnosis were approached. They photographed each member of ELP in black and white, montaging them together with heavy retouching to create an Art Nouveau feel – a movement strongly influenced by Pre-Raphaelite painters. The portrait idea was ELP's, according to Hipgnosis founder Aubrey Powell. He said that the faces were airbrushed to create the look of a painting. The resultant design, showing all three as if they're joined together at the shoulders, is thought to be a visual metaphor for the band's 'one for one, one for all' approach. However, critics thought the band were projecting themselves as gods, leaping on its perceived arrogance. Tellingly perhaps, Hipgnosis never worked for ELP again. Fans, who on the whole had loved the *Tarkus* cover, were non-plussed. Thankfully, the inside of the sleeve was altogether more successful. Photographed in Epping Forest, an ancient beech and oak woodland to the north-east of London, it depicts the band looking relaxed as they strike multiple poses in the autumnal landscape. See if you can spot which member appears the most!

## 'The Endless Enigma Part One' (Emerson, Lake)

Although the band claimed that negative reviews in the music press had little effect on them, Greg Lake's lyrics to *Trilogy's* opening track, 'The Endless Enigma', seems to be in response to the constant mauling the band received at the hand of bitter journalists. Lake was too much of a gentleman to affirm if this was indeed the case but looking at 1972's *Trilogy* tour programme, where sarcastic and scathing reviews from journalists are printed across the inside, the conclusion seems to be that ELP were taking the moral high ground and having the last laugh.

The track opens with the muffled sound of a heartbeat. Jakko M Jakszyk's sleeve notes for his stereo and 5.1 surround sound remixes – which were issued as a double CD and DVDA set in 2015 – claim it was generated by Greg Lake on a bass. However, Carl Palmer's own website says it was generated by himself, playing a bass drum. Listening carefully, there is indeed a slight latency to the rhythm – the kind of effect you get when using a bass drum pedal. And who are we to disagree with ELP's drummer?

There are of course other famous heartbeat effects that open progressive rock albums. However, we should remember that *Trilogy* was released in July 1972, the year before the heartbeat on Pink Floyd's *Dark Side of the Moon*, which was released in March 1973. A nice touch to 'The Endless Enigma' heartbeat is the way it misses a beat, giving the opening seconds of the track an uneasy feel, perhaps representing a tentative birth or awakening. Behind the heartbeat, Keith Emerson's plaintive Moog sketches out a bleak, alien landscape. As the Moog interchanges with startling bursts of Steinway piano – backed by Palmer's reverb-drenched percussion – we're introduced to the distinctive sound of a zurna (listed as a zoukra in *Trilogy's* sleeve notes). Although some have questioned whether Emerson actually played the zurna – a traditional Turkish wind instrument – claiming instead that the sound is a cleverly programmed patch on one of his Moogs. He later revealed that prior to the recording of *Trilogy* he 'haggled and bought the double reeded instrument' while on holiday in Tunisia. He claimed that during the recording sessions, 'It took the effort of blowing up a car tyre to play!'

At around the two minute mark, the band kick in with an impressive blast of archetypal ELP – tight drumming and bass underpinning Emerson's fast Hammond runs. The contrast between the sections works extremely well, emphasising the band's new found confidence in composition and arrangement. The orchestral layering and programming of Emerson's Moogs is something we hadn't heard from the band until this point. It is a primary factor that makes *Trilogy* unlike any other ELP album. On the first album and *Tarkus*, Eddie Offord's engineering skills captured the sound of a band playing live. By contrast, on *Trilogy*, ELP produced music that relied on contemporary studio production techniques with copious amounts of overdubbing and multiple takes.

In the song's first verse, Lake's choirboy vocals sing, 'Your words waste and decay, nothing you say reaches my ears anyway'. There's an edge to his voice that leaves you feeling he really means what he is singing, reinforcing the impression of a man distancing himself from his detractors – 'You never spoke a word of truth', Lake's self penned lyrics barely restrained in their muted anger. As the song builds, the words take on a more abstract feel, becoming that of a man on a quest, turning the other cheek to ignore the malicious jibes. At other times, Lake gives the impression he is in character, almost singing as if he were a god – a fact not lost on the band's detractors!

## 'The Fugue' (Emerson)

As part one of 'The Endless Enigma' fades, Emerson's beautifully recorded Steinway – crisp, clear and powerful – weaves a complex path, backed by dexterous bass playing from Lake. Showing restraint, Palmer reserves his contribution to a few instances of finger cymbals. Although Emerson is the undoubted star of 'The Fugue', Lake's playing deserves mention. It sounds as if Lake is playing a Rickenbacker and not his usual Fender Jazz Bass – the 'Ricky's' treble-heavy sound to the fore, especially on the Jakszyk remix. We know that the ELP bassist bought a 4001 Rickenbacker in San Francisco at around this time, on one of the band's early US tours. Lake was seen playing it at the Melody Maker Poll Awards Concert, at the Oval cricket ground in London on 30 September 1972. According to a brief article in Melody Maker published in the early 1970s, he had the Rickenbacker modified with Fender pick-ups. It was, however, only in his set-up for a short time, the Rickenbacker neck apparently not to his liking, despite its characteristic sound.

As impressive as Lake's playing is – the bass enhancing Emerson's right hand with lines that weave behind the piano, creating depth and colour – it is the keyboard player who is the hero here. Anyone who knows their Bach from their Beethoven (this author most definitely not included!) will know that a fugue is 'a contrapuntal composition in which a short melody or phrase is introduced by one part and successively taken up by others and developed by interweaving the parts.' The name is from the Latin 'fuga' – to avoid or to flee. Emerson, to his credit, always admitted he was not formally classically trained but was nonetheless fascinated by classical composition. 'The Fugue' is his own take at this most exacting musical form, in true Emerson style deviating from the strict structure by infusing jazz alongside classical technique.

He composed 'The Fugue' while on holiday in Sweden, sat at an old upright piano. He claims he had to write out the notation on manuscript before attempting to play it, such was the importance of the construction. Interestingly, a film of Emerson sitting at his piano in his timbered Sussex farmhouse – which is featured on the *Manticore Special* DVD – shows him annotating a manuscript and playing an embryonic version of the piece at almost frantic speed. By the time Emerson came to record 'The Fugue' for *Trilogy*, it was slower and more considered, changed into a beautifully structured piano composition that is the perfect foil to the layered drama of 'The Endless Enigma' that it both precedes and follows.

### 'The Endless Enigma Part Two' (Emerson, Lake)

Although in musical terms 'The Fugue' has very little, if anything, in common with 'The Endless Enigma Part One', the band successfully manage to segue into 'The Endless Enigma Part Two' with stabs of piano, bass and drums taking up the baton. As Palmer plays a repeating four note figure on tubular bells – a refrain that is also taken up on the Hammond – overdubbed Moog bass and the kind of trumpet patch Emerson would later utilise to great effect on *Brain Salad Surgery*, act as a reintroduction to the vocals. The rather obtuse lyrics of 'The Endless Enigma Part Two', are almost as if the words have taken on a different meaning to those in part one . When asked in a Melody Maker interview what the song is about, Lake sidestepped the question by replying that, '...as a rule most of what I write is the result of imagination and not based on actual experiences.' Emerson told audiences on ELP's US tour in August 1972, that 'The Endless Enigma' was inspired by Salvador Dali's painting of the same name. We can assume Emerson composed the music first, asking Lake to add vocals and lyrics later. It has been noted that the theme of the words in 'The Endless Enigma Part Two' is similar to *The Myth of Sisyphus*, a 1942 essay by Albery Camus, the French philosopher, which tells of man's futile search for meaning in the face of a world devoid of God and values.

As Lake's hymn-like vocals tell us he has finally 'begun to see the reason why I'm here', Moog and Hammond fanfares drive the track to a powerful close, synth sirens lending a suitably symphonic ending. The band discovered these layers of Moog and Hammond were impossible to replicate on stage on their 1972 tour. That said, and to their eternal credit, the stripped back version they decided to present was a more than worthy addition to their canon. ELP fans have long lamented the lack of a quality live recording of this version, the only examples existing on bootlegs – three of which were presented as part of the band's *Original Bootleg Series*. The best quality recording is on *Volume One, Disc 5* from Long Beach Arena on 28 July 1971. The other two are on *Volume One, Disc 7* (from Saratoga Performing Arts Centre on 13 August 1972) and on *Volume Two, Disc 1* (from Hammersmith Odeon on 26 November 1972).

## 'From the Beginning' (Lake)

Somewhat lazily dubbed 'Lucky Man part two' by some critics, 'From the Beginning' is in fact an altogether different and more sophisticated song. After the orchestrated bombast of 'The Endless Enigma', this acoustic-led track became their highest performing single, reaching number 39 in the US charts. 'From the Beginning' somewhat surprisingly only became a staple of ELP's live set after their reunion in the early 1990s. Slightly jazzy in tone, with a bossa nova feel, the track centres around Lake's laidback strumming, which is preceded by a wonderful arpeggiated intro. Similar in spirit to 'The Sage' on *Pictures at an Exhibition*, Lake's guitar work is both atmospheric and technically accomplished. In many ways, it is a close cousin to Steve Howe's acoustic opening on 'Roundabout', the two tracks sharing the same key and a similar use of harmonics.

'From the Beginning' is without question an impressive demonstration of Lake's versatility. He not only sings and plays his much-loved Gibson J-200 acoustic guitar, but he also lays down some emotive electric lead guitar, backed by imaginative and melodic bass. The bass here sounds deeper and more rounded than on 'The Endless Enigma', suggesting he is using his Fender Jazz Bass. The lead guitar is particularly impressive, again with a Shadows influence. As the guitar solo ends, Emerson fires up his Moog, matching the mood of the track, yet taking it to another level.

Palmer also deserves a special mention. His creative percussion throughout

'From the Beginning' – particularly the way he softened the sound of his kit by using mallets instead of sticks – gives a the track a relaxed feel, his restrained rhythms cleverly syncing Lake's strumming pattern. 'From the Beginning', although a Greg Lake composition, is a true band effort, a perfect example of their special chemistry.

2015's Jakko Jakszyk re-mix of the *Trilogy* album contains a fascinating bonus track in the form of an alternative take of 'From the Beginning'. Although rougher around the edges and with a different Moog solo, its construction is very close to the original. Emerson plays his solo in a less restrained manner, almost as if this was his first take, the Moog to the fore and unrefined. What is perhaps most noticeable here are Emerson's Moog overdubs, which are louder in the mix. In fact, it is only after hearing this alternative take of 'From the Beginning', then going back and listening to the original, that these synth layers become noticeable. Previously, they blended into the overall soundscape – which was of course the band's intention.

Despite the song's chart success, covers of 'From the Beginning' are few and far between. The US heavy rock band, Dokken, did a version on their 1995 album, *Dysfunctional*. It was also sampled by the singer Amerie on her debut album, *All I Have* – for which Lake received a songwriting credit.

## 'The Sheriff' (Emerson, Lake)

Infamous for Carl Palmer's expletive during his drum intro, 'The Sheriff' tells the tale of Big Kid Josie, a Wild West anti-hero. Unusually for ELP, the song has a narrative, although rather intriguingly it is one without a definitive beginning or end. We're left wondering what happened to Josie, who at the end of the song became 'a legend from the past'. What crime did Josie commit to warrant such attention from the sheriff? Lake's lyrics tell us that Josie watched his friend die at the hands of a lynch mob, but was he innocent and wrongly accused, or did Josie and his friend commit a heinous crime?

The song is a close cousin of 'Jeremy Bender' on *Tarkus* – albeit with a very different subject matter! Initially, the upbeat but darkly overdriven Hammond matches Josie's tale of woe. For the third verse, the tension is increased by a key change, with overdubbed piano giving a theatrical feel, staying just short of pastiche. However, as the song reaches its climax – and a gunshot sound effect signals the demise of the sheriff – Emerson cannot resist increasing the tempo by playing fast vaudeville piano, evoking the sound of a rowdy Wild West bar. As Emerson shows off his immense keyboard technique, he is backed by Palmer's woodblock percussion – a rather comedic touch given Josie's plight and the sheriff's untimely end. Traditionally, the 'honky tonk' sound was achieved by placing tacks onto the end of the piano's hammers, which otherwise struck the strings via felt pads. In the studio, the effect is often aided by detuning some of the piano's strings, creating the sound of an old upright bar piano that hadn't been tuned is a long while. However, engineer Eddie Offord revealed that the sound on 'The Sheriff' was achieved by overdubbing trickery – by recording multi-tracks of piano, some of which were then slowed and sped up, which created a detuning effect.

'The Sheriff' made its live debut in 1972, introduced towards the end of ELP's third North American tour. It was later played as a medley with 'Jeremy Bender' – a version of which is on the triple live *Welcome Back My Friends to the Show That Never Ends*, complete with the fast ragtime section at the end, augmented by comedic piano improvisations by Emerson!

## 'Hoedown' (Copland, Emerson, Lake, Palmer)

Arguably the best known track off the album, 'Hoedown' is an ELP tour de force. Largely based on American composer Aaron Copland's 'Rodeo' – a ballet score – it also borrows from 'Hoe-down', a jazz instrumental by trumpeter Oliver Nelson, from his *The Blues and the Abstract Truth* album. Played live before *Trilogy* had been released, 'Hoedown' quickly became a live favourite and replaced 'The Barbarian' as the band's opening number. It remained in ELP's set until their final gig at The High Voltage Festival in London on 25 July 2010.

Although credited to Copland and the entire band, 'Hoedown' is likely to have been Emerson's 'baby' – a result of his enthusiasm for mixing classical and jazz influences within a rock setting. He greatly admired the American composer, even naming his eldest son Aaron in his honour. The icing on the cake for Emerson was when Copland personally approved of ELP's 'Hoedown' arrangement. Of course it wasn't ELP's only dalliance with a Copland composition, 'Fanfare for the Common Man' from *Works Volume 1* eventually becoming their best known track and a significant hit single.

'Hoedown' begins with a boisterous 'hoover' patch from the Modular Moog, before Emerson plays the main 'Rodeo' theme on his Hammond. As the band join in, Lake and Palmer propel the track at a powerful pace, Emerson taking artistic licence with Copland's original by playing Oliver Nelson's 'Hoe-down' (at 2 minutes 24 seconds), which leads into a section that was greatly expanded on at gigs, Emerson improvising at will, introducing all sorts of musical motifs as he saw fit. It has long been a fallacy that ELP's live gigs were straight run throughs of album tracks. Listening back to the many bootlegs and live recordings of the band, especially those from the early-70s, they thrived on spontaneity and flying by the seat of their pants. When first played on ELP's late 1971 US tour, 'Hoedown' began at a much slower pace, with almost a funky feel. By the time it was being played on their 1974 tour, it was being played at an extreme pace – almost ridiculously so. This is something Greg Lake remarked on in the 1990s, saying that, in hindsight, the band played it much too fast. Interestingly, in the sleeve notes for 2015's *Trilogy* album remix, Jakko Jakszyk tantalisingly mentions that alternative studio versions of 'Hoedown' survive on the original master tapes. One wonders if these were the band experimenting with different speeds. Sadly, none were included as part of the deluxe reissue and we can only hope they will one day gain a release – even if they are only studio jams.

## 'Trilogy' (Emerson, Lake)

The album's title track, which opens side two of the original vinyl album, is a song of contrasts. Opening with an ethereal lone violin patch from the Moog, Emerson's beautifully understated jazzy piano is joined by heartfelt vocals, as Lake tells the tale of a failed relationship. As he sings 'good-bye', waves of piano and bass resolve in a repeating motif that becomes a colossal wall of overdubbed Moogs hitting you like a sledgehammer. Emerson gleefully solos over the top as the band unusually stick rigidly to a repetitive tiff. This is as close to heavy metal as ELP ever got! A rather squeaky Moog fanfare introduces the song's third section, bass, drums, Moog and Hammond interweaving with Lake's impassioned vocals as he paints a more positive outlook on his lost love.

Believed to have been played live just twice in March 1972, *Trilogy* was supposedly axed from the band's set because it required a backing tape to emulate the sound on the album. Carl Palmer had to wear headphones to help keep the live instruments in time with the tape, Lake reportedly unhappy with the complications it gave them on stage. In the informative booklet that accompanies the band's *From the Beginning* box set, Emerson is quoted as saying, 'I don't know why we didn't keep it in our set', bemoaning the fact it was dropped. 'I always felt it could have become an ELP classic' he said, 'but it was never really given the chance on stage'. It is a sentiment most fans would wholeheartedly agree with. No live examples of the band playing 'Trilogy' have ever been issued. The only example can be found on a bootleg recording from the band's performance at Long Beach on 22 March 1972. It is quite possibly the only recorded example in existence. Emerson introduced the song by saying, 'We tried for the first time last night... one of the tracks we want to try is a bit difficult on stage'. He then explains to the audience that they will use a backing track because his monophonic Moog can't play the chords heard on the album. Although the bootleg quality is very rudimentary, the crowd can be heard reacting enthusiastically when the Moog kicks in after the piano intro, then cheering again after the song has finished and Emerson asks them what they thought of the piece. Emerson is correct in grieving the lost opportunity, as 'Trilogy' is one of the band's most ignored tracks. It is also an example of an alternative future for the band had they not decided to record only what they could replicate live, which is what happened on the *Brain Salad Surgery* sessions.

## 'Living Sin' (Emerson, Lake, Palmer)

If 'The Sheriff' is a close cousin of 'Jeremy Bender', then 'Living Sin' is related to 'Time and a Place'. Featuring an unusually deep and almost theatrical vocal from Lake, this is ELP playing straight-ahead rock, the track growling its way through an unsavoury tale of sex. With Emerson's distorted Hammond to the fore, Palmer's drumming is particularly impressive, managing to both meander and lock the track tightly to a sleazy groove. For the most part, Lake's bass closely follows Emerson's left hand, giving an impressive double tracked effect.

Strictly speaking there are no alternative versions of 'Living Sin' – which was incorrectly, and rather unfortunately, titled 'Living Sun' on the otherwise excellent 2015 remix CD issue. Jakko Jakszyk's remix does, however, give the impression of a completely new version. It presents Lake's vocal more upfront, noticeably doubled to left and right in the stereo mix. All instruments are presented far clearer, the drums and Hammond being particularly powerful. If anyone thinks that any of the ELP remixes are commercial gimmicks, think again as this is well worth hearing!

'Living Sin' was the B-side to the 'From the Beginning' hit single in the USA. Somewhat surprisingly, given the track's upbeat nature, it was never performed by ELP live. As a footnote, The Keith Emerson Band, with Marc Bonilla on guitar and vocals, played 'Living Sin' live as part of their live set. It appears on their *Moscow* CD, which was also issued on DVD.

## 'Abaddon's Bolero' (Emerson)

The album's closing track was developed from a synth melody Emerson came up at the end of a band rehearsal. Although it compares only marginally with Ravel's famous 'Bolero' orchestral piece, it retains the same sense of drama and slowly building intensity. According to Emerson, the band initially just jammed it, as he played the theme over and over again. However, as each member of the band gradually added something new, it took on a bolero feel – especially when Palmer, at Emerson's suggestion, played the now-familiar snare drum pattern.

At over 8 minutes long, it is the longest track on *Trilogy*. In a live setting it proved extremely popular, although the layers of instrumentation that Emerson used in the studio caused a few problems. The solution was for Greg Lake to swap his bass for a Mini Moog and a Mellotron – the latter an instrument that Emerson allegedly refused to play himself! It is the only example of Greg Lake playing keyboards with ELP. 'Abaddon's Bolero' was initially played as part of the US tour in March and April 1972 in support of *Trilogy*. Its only performance in the UK was a warm up show at the Capital Theatre in Cardiff on 10 March. However, problems with the Mellotron's tape loops, which kept breaking, led to it being removed from the set – leaving the set extremely light on material from the *Trilogy* album. It was surprisingly reinstated a year later, on the 'Get Me a Ladder' tour, this time as the opening number.

The only live recording from this era of the band playing 'Abaddon's Bolero' is a performance from Louisville Town Hall on 21 April 1972. It is featured on the band's *Original Bootleg Series*. However, as part of the infamous tour with an orchestra in support of *Works*, it was revived yet again – once more as a set opener. This time, Lake had no need to play keyboards as his former role was taken by the full 70-piece orchestra! A recording of this impressive rendition can be heard on *Works Live*, the double CD album released in 1993.

A brand new version of 'Abaddon's Bolero', with the London Philharmonic Orchestra, was recorded during the *Works* era. It was originally released on the promo-only *On Tour With Emerson, Lake & Palmer,* simply titled as

'Bolero'. Retitled 'Abaddon's Bolero', it was issued on Keith Emerson's 1995 solo CD, *Changing States*. Emerson tackled the piece for the last time, again with an orchestra – this time with the Munchner Rundfunkorkester – as part of his Three Fates project alongside Marc Bonilla and Terje Mikkelsen. It was performed at Emerson's last gig, as the opening number, at The Barbican Theatre in London, on 10 July 2015.

For the 2015 *Trilogy* remix, 'Abaddon's Bolero' is arguably one of Jakko Jakszyk's least successful tracks. Although undeniably crisper and with a wider stereo mix, it somehow doesn't have the integrated quality of the original. To be fair, for any long-term fan, the sound of the original mix is always going to be hard to beat – so this could very well be a biased opinion!

## *Trilogy* rarities and bonus tracks

2001 Sanctuary Records edition
Serial number: CMRCD200
A live, previously unreleased version of 'Hoedown' is included as a bonus track as the last track on the CD. This same track is also on 2004's Sanctuary Midline issue (serial number SMRCD058) and two 2011 issues on Sony Music (88697830122) & Legacy (88697830122). It is worth noting that 2004's Sanctuary Midline release also came with an informative twelve page fold-out booklet not present in other issues.

2010 Victory Japanese edition
Serial number: VICP-70151 (reissued in 2012 with the serial number VICP-75060)
The same live version of 'Hoedown' as mentioned above is included as one of three bonus tracks on this Japan-only release, along with 'Take A Pebble'(from 1972's *Mary Y Sol Festival*) and the orchestral version of 'Abaddon's Bolero' (from the promo-only *On Tour with Emerson, Lake & Palmer*). The sleeve is a 7-inch cardboard replica of the original LP.

2015 deluxe edition
Serial numbers: Sony/Legacy/Manticore 88875004902 (UK & Europe release), Razor & Tie 7930183414-2 (USA & Canada release)
The most definite release to-date. CD one is remastered copy of the original album, whereas CD two features King Crimson guitarist Jakko M Jakszyk's new '2015 Stereo Mix' of the album plus an alternative version of 'From the Beginning'. The DVD contains a new 5.1 surround sound mix (also by Jakko M Jakszyk) of all tracks from both CDs.

2016 BMG Music Ltd edition
Serial number: BMGCAT2CD5
This release includes the original remastered album plus Jakko M Jakszyk's 2015 stereo mixes, but not the 5.1 surround sound mixes, or the alternative

version of 'From the Beginning'. It does, however, add the live 'Hoedown' from 2001's Sanctuary Records edition as the final track on CD two – a track missing from the 2015 DVDA editions.

1974 8-Track Quad
Intriguingly, *Trilogy* appeared in 1974's Harrison or Schwann record and tape guide, listed as a Quadraphonic 8-track tape cartridge, with the catalogue number Cotillion QT-9903. This is believed to have never been issued but it is not known whether it was ever mixed for Quad in readiness for release.

# Brain Salad Surgery (1973)

Personnel:
Keith Emerson: Hammond organ, piano, harpsichord, accordian, Moog synthesisers.
Greg Lake: vocals, bass, acoustic guitar, electric guitar
Carl Palmer: drums, percussion & percussion synthesiser
Released: 19 November 1973 (UK), the following month in the USA
Recorded: Advision Studios & Olympic Studios, London, June to September 1973
Highest chart places: 2 in UK, 11 US Billboard 200

After incessantly touring since releasing *Trilogy*, ELP knew they had to get back into the studio to record a new album. Many of the tracks on *Trilogy* had proved difficult to play live due to the number of overdubs made in the studio. This time, the band vowed to do things differently, rehearsing the material in advance to make sure that anything they created could make the transition to the stage. Instead of hiring a rehearsal space, they decided to buy an old cinema in London to create their own facility.

When they decided to form their own record label in early 1973 – which they named Manticore after the fantastical creature that had featured on *Tarkus* – the cinema also became their head office. The band announced that they now, as never before, had both the financial and musical freedom to realise their vision. In true ELP fashion, this included further investment in technology. Moog had recently developed their first polyphonic synthesiser and Emerson was keen to get his hands on one. This would allow him reproduce sounds that hitherto had only been possible by overdubbing in the studio. Both his Mini Moog, which premiered on *Trilogy,* and his original modular Moog system were monophonic, meaning only one note can be played at a time. Chords were therefore only possible by recording and layering notes over one another. Once the new synthesiser, which was a prototype, became part of Emerson's ever-growing arsenal, it had a profound effect on the new material they created. Carl Palmer also got the electronic bug, installing one of the very first percussion synthesisers in his drum kit.

A fascinating record of the band writing and rehearsing at this time was included as part of *The Manticore Special* documentary, aired on the BBC on Boxing Day in 1973 (and in the USA early the following year). This gave a rare behind-the-scenes glimpse at ELP on tour and in rehearsal at the former cinema. The new album was given the working title *Whip Some Skull on Ya* – in typical ELP humour, a euphemism for oral sex. The name was changed at the suggestion of the band's road-manager, Mario Medious, to *Brain Salad Surgery* – the new title taken from the lyrics of the Dr John hit single, 'Right Place, Wrong Time'. With the fellatio theme remaining, albeit somewhat obscurely, the design for the new album's cover by the Swiss artist, H.R. Giger, could go ahead. Without question, this is ELP's most iconic sleeve design, not only because of the artist's striking biomechanical painting but also because of the unique way the front cover opened to reveal the face of a woman – a portrait of Giger's then-girlfriend, Li Tobler. The only change that ELP requested was that Giger airbrush out a rather prominent phallus below the lips of the woman. It was changed into a shaft of light – although not fully obscuring the offending member it has to be said! The two paintings that made up the cover were stolen from an art exhibition in Prague in 2005. They have never been recovered.

Work on the new material took place between the end of 1972 and the first months of 1973. With Lake producing, ELP entered the studio in June, mostly at Olympic Studios in Barnes, West London. The only recording that took place at Advision, where the band had recorded all of their previous studio albums, was the first section of 'Karn Evil 9'. With Eddie Offord increasingly busy with Yes, the *Brain Salad Surgery* sessions were overseen by a different sound engineer, Chris Kimsey. The recording process took four months, followed by mixing in early October, at AIR Studios in London. Greg Lake later said that the sessions were exhausting, 'Nothing came quickly. It really was laborious... like building a house one brick at a time. And sometimes you'd put up a wall and take the whole bloody thing down again.' However, the band's approach was paying dividends in terms of quality, although perhaps at the expense of the improvisation that had marked their earlier efforts. That said, Lake was adamant they had retained the band's 'soul', 'At least that's what we've gone for. I think it generates more energy than previous albums. It's like a collection of emotions you might feel one day – several different emotions.'

Carl Palmer was proud of the effort they put in, 'We spent more time and put more effort into this record than any other we have made. I think if you were to identify one album as being the masterwork of ELP it would have to be *Brain Salad Surgery*. For me, it was our *Sgt. Pepper* moment. We used every recording technique under the sun from recording in the toilet to using custom designed electronic percussion. It's my favourite album by far.' Emerson was no less enthusiastic, 'We felt we needed a bit of time to consider things and not let everything go to our heads. I think it was worth the wait, because a lot of people think *Brain Salad Surgery* is just about the best thing we ever did. The most important thing was the way we were playing together as a band'.

*Brain Salad Surgery* was released in the UK on 19 November 1973. In the UK, it was promoted via a 7-inch flexi disc mounted on the cover of the New Musical Express – the weekly music paper that later in the decade would ironically become one of the band's biggest detractors. On sale nine days before the album was in the shops, this free flexi disc – presented in a miniature facsimile of the album sleeve – gave fans a tantalising preview of the new release, with short snippets of each track. Even better, the disc featured the song 'Brain Salad Surgery' that didn't appear on the album.

The new album peaked at number two in the UK, staying in the charts for 18 weeks. In the USA, it reached number 11 in the Billboard 200. It was in the US album charts for 47 weeks – the longest period for any ELP album. On release, critical response was mixed, although over time reaction has been much kinder and positive. The album is frequently cited as one of the most influential progressive rock albums of all time and is the ELP album most non-diehard fans are likely to own. In the 8 December 1973 edition of Sounds, the UK music weekly, journalist Peter Erskine wrote, 'A lot of people who don't like ELP, like this album. The same goes for me. I don't know whether it's as a result of seeing that BBC film (*The Manticore Special*), or by way of contrast to the intrinsic complexities of the Yes albums, but I can honestly say that I really like all of this. It seems to be their most uncluttered and melodic album to date and certainly their rockiest.'

In the USA, Billboard Magazine were similarly enthusiastic, 'The trio has gone ahead and created a complex, exciting sonic experience which touches on several bases – heady rock, flowing jazz and some zesty pop material.' Almost laughably, in the same publication, the infamous Lester Bangs was less complimentary, saying that technology had taken over their act and the band themselves were little more than robots! Little wonder that Lake later said, 'I suppose it was a bit of a downer when it was released because we had worked such a long time on it, put so much into it and putting touches to it, spent 18 months writing it and we were pissed off that it was dismissed by a few people, as if we had taken three weeks to make it… '.

The North American tour in support of *Brain Salad Surgery* was the band's most extensive yet. It ran from November 1973 until April 1974, with a regular crew of 30 roadies and technicians, plus 15 local men recruited at each venue to comply with union regulations. The band's truck loads of equipment included an impressive lighting rig suspended from a custom-made proscenium frame which the crew erected and dismantled at every venue. According to Greg Lake, the band wanted to take as much of their own equipment from venue to venue to ensure the best possible sound and environment. Gig reviews not only praised the band's flamboyant performance and stage show, they were absolutely astonished at the quality of the sound. This was thanks to a 30-channel desk driving a state-of-the-art Quadraphonic PA system – all 36 tons of it! But not everyone was impressed; Lake's infamous Persian rug, on which he stood whilst playing, came in for widespread scorn. It still does! The story behind the infamous Persian rug is that, apparently, it hid a rubber mat to protect Lake against electric shocks. However, in an ill-judged move, Lake requested that a roadie Hoover the rug before each performance. This gave rise to the rumour that the roadie was employed just for this task. It isn't true of course, but it does illustrate the levels of opulence and excess that surrounded the band at this point. Little wonder they were singled out for derision when punk reared its head a few years later.

Just as excessive, but lending more theatre and musical firepower, was Palmer's incredible two and a half ton stainless steel drum kit – made by British Steel! Mounted on a rotating riser, complete with all manner of percussion, including two massive gongs – one 50 inches in diameter and the other 38 inches – the kit was even equipped with its own lighting system! The whole thing weighed around two and a half tons. Emerson's keyboard kit included Moog's new prototype, the Constellation – a three-keyboard rig, consisting of a 48-note polyphonic synth (the Apollo) with a touch sensitive mono synth (the Lyra) above. The final component – Taurus bass pedals – was placed on the floor and used to generate bass synth parts. The Apollo was primarily used for percussive style keyboard parts, Emerson using it live for 'Benny the Bouncer', 'Jerusalem' and for sections of 'Third Impression'. The Lyra, described by Emerson as like 'a Mini Moog on steroids', was used for lead lines.

In mid-April, the tour finally made its way to Europe, ELP playing a short series of UK dates, including four nights at the Wembley Empire Pool (now known as Wembley Arena). The band were welcomed like conquering heroes. It was the first time a British audience had seen them live since late 1972. It would be even longer before they saw them again.

The *Brain Salad Surgery* tour is documented on the band's triple live *Welcome Back My Friends to the Show That Never Ends, Ladies and Gentlemen...* which was recorded in February 1974 at the Anaheim Convention Center in California. Originally recorded for a 'King Biscuit' radio broadcast in the USA, the band were so impressed with the quality and performance that they had the tracks re-mixed at AIR Studios in London, intending to release them in time to coincide with their British gigs in April. However, the work took a lot longer than expected, finally gaining a release in August.

The band's most famous gig during the *Brain Salad Surgery* era is their performance at the now-legendary California Jam, held at the Ontario Motor Speedway in California on 6 April 1974. Jointly headlined with Deep Purple, ELP's performance was filmed and broadcast live on US television. 44 minutes of this footage is featured as part of the band's *Beyond the Beginning* DVD box set. The California Jam set a number of records – including the loudest amplification system ever used (largely due to Deep Purple's demands) and the highest paid attendance. The California Jam represents the start of the corporatisation of the rock music industry. Slickly run, well promoted and financially sound, it became the model for others to follow.

After the *Brain Salad Surgery* tour, ELP took an extended two and a half year break from touring and recording. When they reconvened for *Works Volume 1*, the tour in support of the new album retained only 'Karn Evil 9, 1st Impression, Part 2' and a short snippet of 'Still... You Turn Me On' during 'Take a Pebble'. When the band reformed in the early-90s, 'Karn Evil 9, 1st Impression, Part 2' opened the set, 'Still... You Turn Me On' also making a return – this time in its entirety as an acoustic number. 'Karn Evil 9' was fittingly the band's opening song at their very last gig – at the High Voltage Festival in July 2010 – Greg Lake's words 'Welcome back my friends to the show that never ends...' ringing out for the very last time.

## 'Jerusalem' (Sir Charles Hubert Hastings Parry, William Blake – arranged by Emerson, Lake, Palmer)

For a band who wrote lyrics on *Tarkus* questioning the existence of God, the choice of 'Jerusalem' as the opening track on *Brain Salad Surgery* may seem strange. We have to remember, however, that 'Jerusalem's place in English culture is a special one. Strictly speaking, 'Jerusalem' is not a hymn as such, but a poem by William Blake set to music composed by Sir Hubert Parry. The poem, entitled Milton, refers to the medieval myth of a young Jesus Christ visiting England accompanied by Joseph of Arimathea. In the poem, Blake also references the Industrial Revolution, unhappy at the direction the country was taking. His 'Dark Satanic Mills' are the factories that were spreading through England (and Britain) at an ever-increasing rate. The 'green and pleasant land' of Blake's youth was fast-disappearing beneath smoke and pollution.

The stirring music composed by Parry has obvious parallels with ELP and is chock-full of pomp and bombast. Emerson in particular would have been aware of 'Jerusalem's' hallowed place during Last Night of the Proms at the Royal Albert Hall – a concert which it always closes, followed by the national anthem. In fact, to many, 'Jerusalem' is England's unofficial anthem, and is considered far more uplifting than the rather dour 'God Save the Queen'.

Emerson had originally tried playing 'Jerusalem' while in The Nice, but it was never rehearsed to his satisfaction. Although Lake was quoted as saying that Blake's words were 'bland' and mostly 'waffle', he did add that 'Jerusalem' had, 'A fantastic melody and something that fitted in with our general vibe'. After ELP released it, he said that, 'I was amazed when people came out with some incredible interpretations. There was one saying it was about the Arab-Jewish fighting at that time. Nothing could have been further from our minds'.

Allegedly, the band wanted to put their version of 'Jerusalem' out as a single in the UK, but the BBC apparently banned it. The reason given was because ELP's interpretation was seen as blasphemy against a much-cherished piece of music. The BBC's decision was heavy handed to say the least. Or was it all simply a clever PR stunt? Releasing singles in the UK was never what ELP were about anyway, their eyes were almost entirely on the USA at the time. Either way, the publicity did the band no harm!

The track is significant for Emerson's playing of the Moog Apollo – the world's first polyphonic synthesiser. Emerson's close relationship with Bob Moog after they'd met at ELP's early-70s gig at Gaelic Park in New York, paid dividends when he was lent the prototype instrument, not only to record *Brain Salad Surgery*, but to take it on tour afterwards. That said, the main 'backing' keyboard on 'Jerusalem' is Emerson's trusty Hammond, double-tracked to give it a fuller sound. The Apollo supplies the track's brassy lead lines and synth bass. Palmer's contribution to 'Jerusalem' should also be praised as he allows the track to breathe by not overplaying. Initially, he restricts himself to orchestral percussion – chimes, timpani and a gong – only coming in on his full kit at the end of the first verse. Throughout, his snare drum work is tight and disciplined, his drums rolls unerringly accurate. Then of course, we have Lake's impressive tenor voice. He sings the track with so much conviction and power that one can only wonder what the BBC were thinking of when they claimed it was disrespectful.

According to Lake, 'We mixed it twice on two, almost 18 hour, sessions … we spent the best part of 36 hours on it.' The version on the original album is the second mix. The first mix can be heard on both 2008's deluxe edition (on Sanctuary Records) and 2014's '40th anniversary' editions (on Sony / Legacy). An impassioned live version of 'Jerusalem' appears on *Welcome Back My Friends* and twice on the *Original Bootleg* series – all recorded in 1974 in support of *Brain Salad Surgery*. It was never played live thereafter. The Apollo synthesiser used to record and play the track live was eventually returned to Moog after the tour ended and never entered production.

## 'Toccata' (Alberto Ginestera)

The Argentinian composer, Alberto Ginestera, had been a huge influence on Emerson when he was writing the opening section of *Tarkus*. However, he claimed he had long wanted to adapt some of the composer's music since first hearing it when on tour with The Nice. 'We were playing with an orchestra in Los Angeles and I was in my dressing room when I heard this incredible music being played on stage by a pianist. It was Ginestera's piano concerto.' When Carl Palmer requested his drum solo be integrated into a piece of music rather than tagged on at the end of a number, Ginestera immediately came to mind. What became 'Toccata' grew out of the fourth movement of the Argentine's piano concerto. The complex composition was laboriously rehearsed, bar by bar, because neither Lake nor Palmer could fully read music.

'Toccata' was actually played live ahead of *Brain Salad Surgery's* release, on ELP's European dates in March 1973. The same gigs also saw the band unveiling 'Karn Evil 9, First Impression' and Lake's ballad, 'Still… You Turn Me On'. It was on one of these dates, while playing in Zurich, Emerson first encountered H.R Giger. 'After I was introduced to him, I went back to the hotel and suggested that Greg and Carl come and meet with him too'. Lake remembered the meeting vividly, 'His house was like a horror movie, filled with his art depicting the grotesque. He was actually a sweet character who really wanted us to use his work – and we agreed he could design our next album cover'.

Because it was already rehearsed, 'Toccata' was one of the first numbers ELP tackled when they recorded *Brain Salad Surgery*. Once in the studio, the band added extra instrumentation, including electronic percussion from Palmer's recently acquired drum synthesiser. At the time, ELP employed an electronic expert called Nick Rose to look after their increasingly complex equipment. Rose came up with a device that Palmer could trigger to create sounds, via small contact mics placed inside his drums. Although relatively crude, it was one of the very first percussion synths. Control was restricted to just volume and changing the octave of the fixed sounds. Despite the limited palette, Palmer crafted them beautifully into his 'Toccata' drum solo – a demonstration of which was given on the BBC TV arts show, *Aquarius*. It is only by seeing Palmer play, that one appreciates how the sounds heard on 'Toccata' are actually generated. Most who heard the track on *Brain Salad Surgery* assumed that the startling electronic soundscapes and noises were created by Emerson.

Without doubt, 'Toccata' is one of the most successful classical adaptations of ELP's career. Justifiably pleased with the result of their recording session, the band realised with horror they hadn't requested permission from Ginestera to release it. When Emerson approached the Argentinian composer's publisher, he was told that Ginestera didn't allow any adaptations of his music. However, the publisher did supply him with Ginestera's phone number. Nervously, Emerson called the composer and spoke to his wife. A meeting was suggested, so the next day Emerson flew to Geneva with ELP's manager, Stewart Young. When they played the track to Ginestera, the composer turned to his wife, exclaiming 'Diabólico!'. Emerson naturally assumed that ELP's adaptation was being given the thumbs down, but the maestro, who didn't speak English, was actually greatly impressed. He said that ELP had captured the essence of his piece like no one else before and that their adaptation was wonderfully menacing. A greatly relieved Emerson was given full permission.

As with most of the tracks on *Brain Salad Surgery*, 'Toccata' was included in the band's live set when they toured in support of the new album. A magnificent version appears on *Welcome Back My Friends*. Sadly, that 1974 tour was the last time it featured in their set.

## 'Still... You Turn Me On' (Lake)

It had become traditional for ELP albums to feature one humorous track plus a Greg Lake acoustic balled. *Brain Salad Surgery* is no except on both counts, and in retrospect said acoustic track, 'Still... You Turn Me On', should have been released as a single. However, despite the fact that earlier Lake songs, 'Lucky Man' and 'From the Beginning', had achieved chart success, the feeling in the band was that they weren't representative of their music. There is of course a counter argument to say that without the attention gained via Lake's songs, ELP wouldn't have had the same degree of album success. It should also be noted that Palmer doesn't feature on 'Still... You Turn Me On' – a fact that may have influenced their decision. Lake, for his part, respected the view of his bandmates and the track remained solely an album track.

Lake's somewhat abstract lyrics for 'Still... You Turn Me On' have caused some discussion over the years. In attempting to explain what they mean, he once said, 'When the audience looks up on the stage they see a star, but a star is just a perception, so it was a concept that I was trying to voice, but in a romantic way.' He was apparently describing how he felt about female fans in the audience at ELP gigs! One criticism that could be levelled at the song is that on *Brain Salad Surgery* it is rather over-embellished with layers of overdubs.

By contrast, the version on *Welcome Back My Friends* is beautifully simple and heartfelt. Three other versions from that tour also feature on the *Original Bootleg Series*, along with later performances from the early-1990s.

When the song was played live in Europe in the Spring of 1974, before the band recorded *Brain Salad Surgery*, the audience was treated to a 'work in progress'. The first two verses were the same, but thereafter the song was very different – including a final, more uptempo verse that never made it onto the album. Lake even threw in a musical reference to what would eventually become 'Closer to Believing' on *Works Volume 1*.

As with 'Jerusalem', an alternative first mix was issued as part of both 2008's deluxe edition and 2014's '40th anniversary' edition. This has a different, more tentative, vocal take and stronger electric guitar.

## 'Benny the Bouncer' (Emerson, Lake, Sinfield)

On previous ELP albums, Emerson had played this kind of good time bar room boogie on a piano. However, the Moog Apollo's appearance in his keyboard arsenal influenced a far more experimental approach. Seizing the chance to test his new keyboard, he uses it to play the intro and first verse, giving 'Benny the Bouncer' a totally different kind of feel. In many ways, its use predates 1980s synth pop music – something that many of the keyboard stars from that era, such as Howard Jones, would readily admit to. As with most Emerson-led compositions, the music came first, followed by the lyrics and vocal melody. For 'Benny the Bouncer', Lake called his former King Crimson bandmate, Pete Sinfield, for assistance with the lyrics. Apparently, this was in exchange for Lake helping out with Sinfield's debut album, *Still*. As a result, Lake is listed an associate producer credit for Sinfield's album as well as lending a hand with vocals and electric guitar.

The lyrics that Sinfield came up with tell the story of Benny, a Cockney bouncer – which Lake half-sung, half-narrated, in a sleazy East End of London accent. In Sinfield's tongue-in-cheek tale, Benny comes up against a nasty punter, Savage Sid, and is killed. He then becomes the bouncer at St Peter's Gate. According to Sinfield, 'I'd always had a fondness for Cockney music hall songs, so we wrote about 'Benny the Bouncer'... and we wrote it very fast!' Lake claimed that the Benny character was based on a bouncer he'd known at Salisbury City Hall. 'He was fucking huge! He must have been six foot three... no one would ever dare say anything to him. But he is 'Benny the Bouncer' and the Palais De Danse is Salisbury City Hall.'

For the backing track, Emerson cleverly layers the keyboards by introducing a honky tonk piano on the first chorus. After Lake sings 'One hell of a fight!' he takes a ridiculously fast honky-tonk piano solo, complete with fight sound effects of shouting and breaking glasses. The band seemed determined to have fun with this one! If you listen very carefully, you can even hear faint snatches of electric guitar in the mix – possibly spill from an earlier track-bounce, as it doesn't really sound as if it should be there. With Benny dispatched to heaven

('The end of a ted') this short song reaches its climax, although in typical Emerson fashion it is only a false ending, allowing his bar room piano to return for one final comedic flourish.

'Benny the Bouncer' is the only track on *Brain Salad Surgery* that doesn't appear on *Welcome Back My Friends* – for unknown reasons. It is known that ELP played the song regularly on their 1974 tour – and it was actually performed on the night the album was recorded. Who knows, if *Welcome Back My Friends* is ever given the deluxe treatment, maybe it will be added as a bonus track?

## 'Karn Evil 9 1st Impression' Part 1 (Emerson, Lake)

The last track on side one of the original vinyl album, 'Karn Evil 9, 1st Impression, Part 1' was the very first track the band recorded at Olympic Studios in June 1973. Road tested on their 'Get Me a Ladder' tour in Europe in the Spring of 1973, the track was originally going to be called 'Ganton 9' and was Keith Emerson's future vision for a planet where anything goes. Pete Sinfield laughed when he heard the name, telling the band they couldn't call it that because, 'there's a Ganton Street in Soho, just down the road'! So he convinced the band to rename it 'Karn Evil 9' instead – a play on the word 'carnival'.

The first section of this iconic ELP track has its origins in a piece of music Emerson had written as an exercise. According to Emerson this was 'The logical extension of the musical path we had taken with *Tarkus*; I decided I wanted to write a musical exercise in counterpoint. But after the first movement had come together I gave up on the idea.' When he played it to his bandmates they agreed it was clever in a musical sense but commented, 'Can we get on with the song now'! Getting on with it meant working through the manuscript Emerson had prepared – his preferred way of working despite Lake's inability to read music. By this stage, Palmer could read to a certain extent, classical timpani lessons at London's Guildhall School of Music having paid dividends. Jamming the track, which is how most bands develop ideas, was not to Emerson's liking, 'Occasionally we used to make music up from blues jams, but I didn't always think that it was satisfactory.' The band initially rehearsed 'Karn Evil 9' in their personal rehearsal studio – in the former projection room at their converted cinema in Fulham. The main rehearsal space, using the cinema's stage, was usually rented out to other bands such as Led Zeppelin and Jethro Tull. For some reason, the larger space wasn't being used so they temporarily moved into it. According to Palmer, this was the big moment for 'Karn Evil 9', 'Once on the big stage it just took off!'

In terms of lyrical content, at the beginning of the 'Karn Evil 9 1st Impression, Part 1', Lake sings in the first person, describing a world set in the near future. An uncaring malaise that has taken over mankind, creating a selfish and materialistic world where the innocent suffer. Lake's lyrics prophesise famine and refugees, as an apathetic world watches through the eyes of the media. He could easily be singing about the world in the 21st century. Then, with parallels to the dystopian worlds he sang about in 'Tarkus' and 'The Endless Enigma', he hints he could be a potential saviour: 'I'll be there, to heal their sorrow, to beg and borrow, fight tomorrow'. His words acting as a rallying call and a plea for people to join him to help save the world. The viewpoint suddenly shifts to that of a fairground barker cajoling people to 'come inside' and 'see the show'. This isn't your everyday funfair, Lake's lyrics describing a Ray Bradbury-esque world where entertainment is king, the more shocking the better. Sex, violence, religion and bloodsport are all on display at this future shock carnival – a voyeuristic society where even the environment has been reduced to entertainment. 'There behind the glass stands a real blade of grass' is a chilling line that echoes a topic that has grown immeasurably since Lake first sang these words in 1973. Lake said of 'Karn Evil 9', 'Some of the lyrics are surreal, but then I felt that there is something that needed to be said, for instance, like the way the media makes money from photographing people suffering. That is just a strange reality of the way human beings are'. To modern ears, there is nothing surreal in what Lakes sings. He is describing the world we live in.

There is little doubt that 'Karn Evil 9, 1st Impression' Part 1 is the essential core sound of ELP – bass, drums and Hammond, accentuated by Moog fanfares. Distilled to the point of perfection, it is a credit to the band that overdubs are kept to a minimum. And although the composition can hardly be said to be simple, an effort does seem to have been made to pare things back compared to the studio excess of *Trilogy*. In particular, Lake's bass playing is simpler and more direct than previously. Having been burned by the ambitious band orchestration on *Trilogy*, perhaps the challenge of singing whilst playing complex lines was now something he wished to avoid. In terms of equipment, we know that on *Brain Salad Surgery* Lake was back to using a Fender Jazz bass, which he was quick to praise, 'The Fender offers an excellent combination of design and versatility. The neck is also nimble and quick to get around on. In ELP, I have to cover a lot of different parts and some of them are very fast. If you play something like 'Tarkus', it's shifting along at quite a speed. A big neck would be too slow and awkward to deal with. The Fender neck lets me move around to match the pace of the music. It also has a beautiful, resonant low end. I always tried to sound the Jazz like the bass end of Keith's Steinway piano, so I favoured an ultra-clean hi-fi tone. It has an ash body and a slab neck, all of which adds up to near perfection in a bass guitar. It's hard to improve on it'. That said, the bass he favoured when ELP went out on tour in support of the album was a Gibson Ripper, which he would later swap for an Alembic – the ultimate rock star bass of the 1970s.

Although Emerson leads the way on 'Karn Evil 9, 1st Impression' Part 1, Palmer pulls no punches whatsoever. The entire track is an impressive workout between Emerson's Hammond and some extremely complex drum patterns – a comment that is probably true of the entire album. '1st Impression' moves

Nic Dartnell's iconic cover painting for ELP's debut album seems to cry out for a gatefold sleeve. It is a shame that the only gatefold version – with a band portrait taking up the entire inside – was issued to accompany the first German pressing, as seen here. *(BMG / Author's own collection. Photo: Laura Goode / Hop House Design.)*

A full page photograph of Carl Palmer from ELP's very first tour programme. *(Author's own collection)*

Carl Palmer in a characteristic blur of speed during an early gig – as featured on the band's *Masters From The Vault* DVD. *(Intense Media Ltd)*

The inside gatefold of *Pictures at an Exhibition* plus, in front, the Russian edition of the album. William Neal's paintings are in ornate frames he sourced from junk shops. He hung the paintings on the wooden panelled walls of Hammersmith Town Hall, before art directing a photographer to capture the scene. The all-white painting for 'Promenade' actually depicts a white dove in relief on a white background – an homage to Nic Dartnell's painting for ELP's debut album. Although the dove was invisible on the photographs, Neal decided leave it as is. *(BMG / Author's own collection. Photo: Laura Goode / Hop House Design.)*

William Neal's original *Tarkus* cover design in its raw state. Note that the front, on the right, featured just had the band's name, with the tail of the Tarkus only just visible. To see the whole Tarkus, you'd have to open the gatefold or flip it over. Although this design was rejected, the band loved Neal's Tarkus illustration, asking him to place it more prominently on the front cover, which of course became the final and much-loved design. *(William Neal)*

This 1971 US tour ad shows William Neal's original illustration for the *Tarkus* album cover. On seeing it, the band thought the creature looked too friendly and asked Neal to make it look 'meaner'. Neal has often said he preferred this version to the one eventually used on the album cover. *(William Neal. Author's own collection.)*

William Neal's front cover and inside gatefold for *Tarkus*. The sleeve tells the Tarkus story, a concept Neal developed with the band. *(BMG / Author's own collection. Photo: Laura Goode / Hop House Design.)*

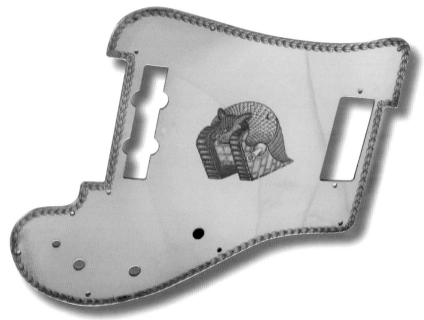

This beautifully engraved chrome *Tarkus* scratch-plate was destined for Greg Lake's Rickenbacker 4001 bass guitar. However, a mistake made when cutting it to shape meant it didn't fit! The large holes evidence Lake's conversion of the Rickenbacker to accommodate his favoured Fender Jazz pick-up in the bridge position. Lake only briefly used the Rickenbacker – sadly minus this wonderful work of art – most notably at 1972's *Melody Maker* Poll Winners gig at The Oval, in London.
*(Author's own collection. Photo: Laura Goode / Hop House Design.)*

After the success of the *Tarkus* sleeve, *Trilogy* was something of a disappointment – despite being designed by the famous Hipgnosis team. William Neal was originally commissioned to create the design but the band didn't like the ideas he came up with. The Hipgnosis cover is meant to have a Pre-Raphaelite feel, although critics thought it was an arrogant attempt by the band to portray themselves as musical gods. The inside gatefold shows multiple images of the band shot at Epping Forest. For some reason, there are only six Keith Emersons and Carl Palmers but eight Greg Lakes! *(Sony / Author's own collection. Photo: Laura Goode / Hop House Design.)*

Among the most intriguing audio formats for ELP collectors are the band's 8-track cartridge releases. Because of the way the cartridges play, it often necessitated a different running order – as on this example of *Trilogy*. Rarest of all is a Quad-8 issue of *Welcome Back*, which replicates the band's famed quadraphonic live sound from their 1974 tour. As *Welcome Back* has never been released in 5.1 surround sound, the original Quad-8 cartridge is the only way for fans to hear this quadraphonic mix. *(Author's own collection. Photo: Laura Goode / Hop House Design.)*

The front cover of the *New Musical Express* from 10 November 1973, complete with the free 'flexi disk' that includes snippets from ELP's *Brain Salad Surgery* album, plus the track of the same name. Until *Works Volume 2* was released, this was the only way for fans to hear the *Brain Salad Surgery* track. *(Author's own collection. Photo: Laura Goode / Hop House Design.)*

*Brain Salad Surgery* was ELP's first release on their own Manticore label. Although the famed cover was illustrated by H. R. Giger. the unique triptych sleeve was devised by the Italian art director, Fabio Nicoli. *(BMG / Author's own collection. Photo: Laura Goode / Hop House Design.)*

ELP's four dates in April 1974, at the Empire Pool, Wembley (now known as Wembley Arena) were the band's first UK gigs for over a year. The short tour, which also included gigs in Liverpool and Stoke, was celebrated by this special programme. Note the misspelling of Emerson on the ticket! *(Author's own collection. Photo: Laura Goode / Hop House Design.)*

The triple vinyl *Live in Italy May 1973* was part of 2017's lavish *Fanfare 1970-1997* box set. Recorded at the Studio Flaminio, Rome, and the Velodromo Vigorelli, Milan, these previously unreleased gigs captures ELP on their 'Get Me a Ladder' European tour in 1973. The tour was notable for previewing tracks which would be released on *Brain Salad Surgery* later that year. *(BMG / Author's own collection. Photo: Laura Goode / Hop House Design.)*

Surrounded by Bedouin tribesmen and their children, this official Manticore photograph was issued to coincide with Greg Lake's 1975 hit single, 'I Believe In Father Christmas'. The single reached number two in the UK charts, only kept off the top slot by Queen's 'Bohemian Rhapsody'. *(Manticore / Warner Bros / Author's own collection.)*

**GREG LAKE**

This seldom seen Manticore press photograph of Greg Lake shows him playing his favoured Fender Jazz Bass. However, it is the Fender Telecaster in the background that is of most interest. This is the guitar he used on the band's Tarkus recording session, notably on 'Battlefield'. *(Manticore / Warner Bros / Author's own collection.)*

**GREG LAKE**

Keith Emerson made an appearance on famed jazz pianist Oscar Petersen's BBC TV show to promote 'Honky Tonk Train Blues'. Together with a prestigious slot on Top of the Pops, it helped propel the single to number 21 in the UK charts. Written by Meade Lux Lewis, this up-tempo piano instrumental was originally intended to be part of an Emerson solo release in the early 1970s. *(BBC TV)*

This official ELP press shot was issued to promote the band's North American tour in support of *Works Volume 1*. Recent years have seen a number of live recordings from this tour that feature the band as a trio, minus the infamous orchestra. *(Warner Bros / Author's own collection.)*

The rear cover of the *Works* tour programme from 1977. While the band were rehearsing in the basement of the Olympic Stadium in Montreal, a freak heavy snowfall covered the city. Taking advantage of the conditions, the band's crew lugged their equipment upstairs into the stadium so they could be videoed miming to 'Fanfare for the Common Man'. According to Greg Lake, it was so cold that they could only manage to record for around two minutes at a time, before retreating downstairs to warm their hands! *(Author's own collection.)*

The tasteful design and typography of the two Works albums reflected ELP's desire to be taken seriously as composers and performers. To the front is a promotional album issued to radio stations, containing edited versions of selected tracks from *Works Volume 1*. *(BMG / Author's own collection. Photo: Laura Goode / Hop House Design.)*

This promo album was issued to radio stations in North America during ELP's 1977 tour in support of *Works Volume 1*. The album features interviews with the band, the then-unreleased 'Tiger in a Spotlight' and an orchestral version of 'Bolero'. The former would eventually be released on *Works Volume 2*, whereas the latter wouldn't see a release until it appeared on Keith Emerson's *Changing States* CD in 1995. *(Author's own collection. Photo: Laura Goode / Hop House Design.)*

The programme for ELP's North American tour in 1977 and 1978 in support of *Works Volume 1*. The band performed the vast majority of the dates as a trio, the orchestra sadly axed after just two weeks. With and without the orchestra, a highlight of the tour – and indeed the album – was 'Pirates', arguably ELP's last great epic. *(Author's own collection. Photo: Laura Goode / Hop House Design.)*

By the time ELP recorded their *Live '77* video (later released as *Works Orchestral Tour*), Greg Lake was playing an impressive array of Alembic guitars and basses – 'de rigeur' instruments for top rock stars in the late-1970s. Lake's most famous Alembic is an 8-string bass, as featured on 'Fanfare For The Common Man'. *(Warner Bros.)*

The inside sleeve of *In Concert*, the live album of the *Works* tour that was released in 1979. The photograph shows the incredible amount of personnel and equipment required to take the ill-fated 70-piece orchestra on the road. *(WEA / Author's own collection.)*

The infamous *Love Beach*, ELP's last album of the 1970s. All three members would later regret the cover photograph, which made the band more like the Bee Gees than progressive rock heroes. *(BMG / Author's own collection. Photo: Laura Goode / Hop House Design.)*

The front and back cover of *Black Moon - Rough Mixes*, a CD only available to fans who bought the band's luxurious *Fanfare 1970-1997* box set via Pledge Music. The tracks on this CD are rawer than the slicker Mark Mancina-produced mixes heard on the final album. Note the different running order to *Black Moon* and that the opening track, 'Frontiers', was yet to be renamed 'Changing States'. The only *Black Moon* track not present here is 'Footsteps in the Snow. *(JVC Kenwood Victor Entertainment. Author's own collection.)*

The performance captured on ELP's *Live at The Royal Albert Hall* DVD was Keith Emerson's first gig at the venue since he'd been banned for burning the American flag whilst playing there with The Nice on 26 June 1968. The intervening years showed he'd lost none of his flair for showmanship, these gigs featuring him spraying 'ELP' graffiti onto a brick wall behind his racks of keyboards. *(Membran Music Ltd / Beckmann Communication / Livezone.)*

A still from *Live at The Royal Albert Hall* DVD showing Emerson abusing his Hammond organ during 'Rondo' – which had been the band's encore since they formed in 1970. Fittingly, 'Rondo' was the last number the band ever played together, at London's High Voltage Festival in 2010. *(Membran Music Ltd / Beckmann Communication / Livezone)*

*In The Hot Seat*, ELP's last studio album, wasn't released on vinyl until 2017, as part of BMG/ Manticore's reissuing of the band's entire back catalogue. Each release came with a note from Greg Lake explaining why they were produced on 140gsm vinyl as opposed to the much-touted heavier 180gsm. *(BMG / Author's own collection. Photo: Laura Goode / Hop House Design.)*

Released as part of Record Store Day in 2011, ELP released this limited edition vinyl-only album. Side one features *Tarkus* and side two has a cut down version of *Pictures at an Exhibition* – both recorded live at the band's Mar Y Sol Festival performance in 1972. *(Author's own collection. Photo: Laura Goode / Hop House Design.)*

The four volumes of *The Original Bootleg Series* are now collector's items. Each box featuring multiple CDs of live recordings from 1971 to 1993. Housed in sleeves that emulate bootlegs from the vinyl era, the sound quality varies from stereo soundboard recordings to rudimentary audio captured by fans at gigs. Listening to all 28 CDs is a fascinating experience – an accurate warts-and-all snapshot of ELP's live career. *(Author's own collection. Photo: Laura Goode / Hop House Design.)*

Limited to just 3,000 copies, 2017's *Fanfare 1970-1997* box set features 18 CDs, including all of the band's studio albums and five unreleased live performances, a Blu-ray of 5.1 surround sound mixes and high res audio, the tripe vinyl *Live in Italy May 1973*, two 7" singles, replica tour programmes and posters, plus a hard back book. However, none of the studio albums feature any bonus tracks.
*(BMG / Author's own collection. Photo: Laura Goode / Hop House Design.)*

ahead relentlessly, never letting up for a second. It is an exhilarating ride musically and lyrically, reaching a crescendo towards the end of side one when Lake's electric guitar takes over as the lead instrument, producing salvo after salvo of uplifting anthemic licks before giving way to a hypnotic sequence from Emerson's Moog.

### 'Karn Evil 9, 1st Impression, Part 2' (Emerson, Lake, Sinfield)
On the original vinyl album, the Moog sequence ended side one and continued when you flipped the LP over and dropped the needle onto side two – a neat audio trick that became a much-loved favourite of hi-fi enthusiasts. Played digitally and on CD, the effect is not quite the same, although any lingering disappointment (assuming one remembers the thrill of playing the original LP!) is swept aside when the sequence, now accompanied by Palmer's tambourine, is joined by Lake vocals as he sings the iconic, 'Welcome back my friends to the show that never ends...'. Peter Sinfield, who helped Lake with the lyrics, is justifiably proud of his work on the track. 'I wrote 'Soon the Gypsy Queen in a glaze of Vaseline, will perform on guillotine, what a scene!' because 'vaseline' rhymes so well with queen. Greg thought it was amusing and he liked singing it.' Sinfield's way with words earned him special credit on the *Brain Salad Surgery* album sleeve – 'Many thanks and a garland of Martian fire flowers to Pete Sinfield for his collaboration on the lyrics for 'Benny the Bouncer' and 'Karn Evil 9'.'

Musically, '1st Impression, Part 2' is no less imposing than 'Part 1'. At just 4 minutes and 45 seconds, in many ways it encapsulates ELP's entire musical approach. With Lake's guitar again to the fore, Palmer's incessantly inventive drumming and Emerson's rich Hammond and Moog orchestration, the track powers over the finish line for its 'See the show' conclusion. Splitting 'Karn Evil 9, 1st Impression, Part 1' and 'Part 2' onto separate sides of the vinyl album paid dividends when US FM radio, recognising 'Part 2' as a separate track, began to give it serious airplay even though it was never released as a single. It is the only ELP track of this era, apart from Lake's acoustic ballads, to be played on the radio in this way. As a result, sales of the *Brain Salad Surgery* album soared.

### 'Karn Evil 9, 2nd Impression' (Emerson)
Less of an easy mainstream rock listen, 'Karn Evil 9, 2nd Impression' was originally written by Emerson for a piano concerto. It relieves the symphonic pomp, marking a return to the more eclectic spirit of ELP's debut album. Opening with a complex weave of bass, drums and piano, Emerson introduces a Caribbean steel drum patch on his Minimoog to play a loose frantic interpretation of jazz saxophonist Sonny Rollins' *St. Thomas*. Recorded at Advision Studios in August 1973, the breakneck speed eventually fades to a gentler and more considered piano-led section, Lake taking the opportunity to play some creative electric bass behind a series of startling percussive effects. As

65

the pace inevitably increases once more, Emerson layers flourish after flourish of virtuoso piano, taking this seven minute jazz-heavy track to a short sharp finale. Taken a face value, there seems to be little thematic link between the '2nd Impression' and the rest of 'Karn Evil 9', although Emerson's explanation was that the piece 'expresses the restlessness of our times and the speed of change'. The value of 'Karn Evil 9, 2nd Impression' is that it adds a dash of salt to what otherwise could have been an over-sweet pudding. It definitely benefits from repeated playing and the temptation to skip this more 'difficult' track when listening to *Brain Salad Surgery* as a whole is something that should be discouraged.

## 'Karn Evil 9, 3rd Impression' (Emerson, Lake, Sinfield)

Without pausing for breath, not even allowing the last piano chord of the '2nd Impression' to fade, Lake's distorted bass and Emerson's Moog fanfare introduce the triumphant 'Karn Evil 9, 3rd Impression'. With one of Lake's finest vocal melodies, the lyrics tell of an impending war between man and machines. Written around a Sinfield concept, the theme of computers taking over mankind was a subject close to the lyricist's heart. 'I spent six years in computers before I became a songwriter', he explained. 'I've always been fascinated with artificial intelligence versus natural intelligence because one is born of the other, and it goes around in an odd circle.'

Lake later expounded on the idea, 'The whole premise of 'Karn Evil 9' was the influence that computers would have upon civilisation' – a prophetic viewpoint bearing in mind that *Brain Salad Surgery* was written and recorded in 1973, a time when nobody had a personal computer. Emerson notes, with some irony, 'It was the start of computer technology and already we were being accused of using them in our instrumentation to the point that some people actually believed that when we played live onstage, it wasn't actually us! That's why I programmed the Moog to get into a sequence at the end of 'Karn Evil 9' when we played live. I had the Moog turn around, face the audience and blow up while we left the stage. It was like saying – this is computer technology and it is taking over.'

Emerson described 'Karn Evil 9, 3rd Impression' as being very 'Elgar-ish', which is an accurate description of the track's swaggering, imperialistic British-flavoured pomp. As Lake's vocals remonstrate with the computer – Emerson's voice run through the Moog's ring modulator – the 'maps of war' are drawn between mankind and computer-controlled machines in a fanfare of chest-beating Moogs. The war is announced by a passionate bluesy Hammond solo, before the sound of Moogs make their presence felt in a series of exchanges with a chattering Hammond. Does Emerson's organic Hammond represent mankind and the laser-like Moogs represent computers? When Lake's proud vocals trumpet mankind's victory, 'Rejoice, Glory is ours', then arrogantly boasts, 'I am all there is', the voice of the computer chillingly interjects, 'I am perfect, are you?'. The track ends with a Moog playing a taught sequence which increases in speed as it cascades from ear to ear across the stereo mix. Mankind had spoken too soon, the machines cannot be defeated.

On the super-deluxe '40th Anniversary' box set of *Brain Salad Surgery*, one of the many bonus tracks is of ELP running through 'Karn Evil 9 3rd Impression' in the studio. This could be the band playing the track in preparation for recording it, or just a rehearsal tape. A lack of vocals tends to favour the former. Nonetheless, it is an invaluable glimpse of the band at work, revealing hitherto unheard facets of the track and emphasising what astonishing musicians they were. It is a shame that similar versions of the 1st and 2nd Impressions don't also exist.

## *Brain Salad Surgery* rarities and bonus tracks

1993 US Victory digipak edition
Serial number: 383 480 015-2
A mini replica of the original album sleeve, complete with the die-cut and poster.

1996 US Rhino lenticular cover edition
Serial number: R2 72459
Presented in a lenticular 3d-effect cover, in lieu of the die-cut original, this remastered version comes with a bonus track – a series of audio interviews with the band and Peter Sinfield on the making of *Brain Salad Surgery*. Also included is a 20-page booklet with track information and an essay on the band and album.

1997 UK Castle Communications LP plus single
Serial number: ORRLP 002
Limited to 5,000 copies, this remastered 160gm vinyl edition comes with a one-sided 7 inch single featuring the track 'Brain Salad Surgery'. The LP has a facsimile of the original die-cut sleeve plus a UK obi strip.

2000 US Rhino DVD-Audio edition
Serial number: R9 75980
Presented in an oversized jewel case, this special issue was mixed and mastered specifically for DVD-Audio, presenting the *Brain Salad Surgery* tracks in 5.1 surround sound – plus 'Lucky Man' from ELP's debut album. As a bonus, a video section of the DVD includes excerpts from the *Manticore Special* documentary plus 'Lucky Man' live from 1992. A 20-page booklet is also included – the same as the one in the 1996 'lenticular cover' edition.

2001 UK Castle Music edition
Serial number: CMRCD201
Remastered, this UK edition includes full versions of 'Brain Salad Surgery' (the

track) and 'When the Apple Blossoms Bloom in the Windmills of Your Mind I'll Be Your Valentine' – both recorded during the *Brain Salad Surgery* album sessions – plus the *Brain Salad Surgery* excerpts from the original New Music Express flexi disc.

2002 UK Castle Music miniature LP edition
Serial number: CMTCD433
As the 2001 edition but in a miniature replica of the original LP and its poster insert.

2008 Sanctuary deluxe edition
Serial number: 5308195
Remastered double CD & 1 x SACD set. The original album on CD1, with bonus tracks on CD2 – 'Brain Salad Surgery', 'When the Apple Blossoms Bloom in the Windmills of Your Mind I'll Be Your Valentine', 'Karn Evil 9 3rd Impression' (original backing track), 'Jerusalem' (first mix), 'Still… You Turn Me On' (first mix), 'Toccata' (first mix), 'Karn Evil 9' (full version, parts 1 to 3, alternative '35th Anniversary' versions), plus the *Brain Salad Surgery* excerpts from the original New Music Express flexi disc. The SACD contains 5.1 surround sound mixes of the original album. Includes a 16-page colour booklet telling the story of *Brain Salad Surgery*.

2013 US Razor & Tie 180g '40th anniversary' LP
Serial number: 7930183415-1
180g audiophile vinyl edition of the original album – including die-cut sleeve and poster – to celebrate the 40th Anniversary of *Brain Salad Surgery's* release.

2013 US Razor & Tie 180g '40th anniversary' LP picture disc
Serial number: 7930183415-1
Limited to 2000 copies, this picture disc was a special release for the US Record Store Day.

2014 UK & Europe '40th anniversary' super deluxe box set
Serial number: 88883772862 (Sony, Legacy, Manticore)
The deluxe LP-sized box set includes triple CDs, double DVDs and single LP. The first CD is a remastered version of the original album, whereas CD 2 was the 'Alternative *Brain Salad Surgery*' – 'Karn Evil 9 3rd Impression' (original backing track), 'Jerusalem' (first mix), 'Still… You Turn Me On' (first mix), 'Toccata' (alternative version), 'Karn Evil 9' (full version, parts 1 to 3, alternative '35th Anniversary' versions), the NME *Brain Salad Surgery* flexi disc, 'When the Apple Blossoms Bloom in the Windmills of Your Mind I'll Be Your Valentine', 'Brain Salad Surgery', 'Brain Salad Surgery' (a 'live in the studio' version) and 'Karn Evil 9 3rd Impression' (a 'live in the studio' version minus vocals). CD3 is new stereo versions of the original album. The first DVD,

a DVD-Audio disc, contains the 'Super Sonic *Brain Salad Surgery'* (new stereo mixes in high quality audio and in 5.1 surround sound) plus the 'Original Stereo Mix'(the original stereo mixes in high quality audio and in 5.1 surround sound). DVD 2 is the *Manticore Special* documentary. The LP is the original album, pressed on 180gm vinyl, oddly not presented the original die-cut sleeve but slipped inside in a special gatefold cover that also houses the CDs and DVDs. Included is a comprehensive 20-page LP-sized booklet, with an essay by Chris Welch, the ex-Melody Maker journalist and a champion of the band. Also included are quotes from the band themselves, archive imagery and ephemera, plus notes from Jakko Jakszyk on his 5.1 mixes. Note that these new 5.1 mixes are different to the ones on the earlier '35th Anniversary' sets.

The 40th Anniversary issues also included a 'deluxe' edition consisting of double CDs (the original album plus the 'Alternative *Brain Salad Surgery'*) and a DVD-A (the 'Super Sonic *Brain Salad Surgery')*. This came with a 16-page booklet, the discs housed in an 8-panel roll fold digitally pack. It was also issued in a less extensive standard format, as a double CD (the original album plus the 'Alternative *Brain Salad Surgery'*) with a 12-page booklet.

# Works Volume 1 (1977)

Personnel:
Keith Emerson: Yamaha GX-1 polyphonic synthesiser, Steinway piano, Hammond B3, Moog synthesisers
Greg Lake: vocals, Bass, Acoustic Guitar, Electric Guitar
Carl Palmer: drums, Percussion, Vibraphone.
Additional musicians:
Joe Walsh, Andy Hendkriksen, James Blades, John Timperley plus an unknown number of session musicians who played on side two (Greg Lake) and side three (Carl Palmer).
Orchestras:
London Philharmonic Orchestra (conducted by John Mayer), The Orchestra de l'Opera de Paris (conducted by Godfrey Salmon)
Released: 17 March 1977
Recorded: Mountain Studios, Switzerland & EMI Studios, Paris
Highest chart places: 9 in UK, 12 US Billboard 200

By the time ELP had played their last gig of the *Brain Salad Surgery* tour on 24 August 1974, all three members were exhausted, both creatively and physically. Having been on the road almost non-stop since the Summer of 1970, they decided to take a break to recharge their batteries and spend time with their families. The common misconception is that ELP were then idle until they released *Works Volume 1*, over two and a half years later. In fact, all three members were back in the studio the following year, recording material for planned solo releases. They also rehearsed and recorded as a band, although only one track has ever been released from these sessions – the instrumental, 'Bo Diddley', which was eventually released as part of the *Return of the Manticore* box set in 1994.

In a November 1974 Circus magazine interview with Mario Medious, ELP's US promotion guru, it was reported that Emerson and Palmer's solo albums were 'fifty percent complete'. Medious went on to say that Lake had written an album's worth of material but had so far only recorded one track, 'C'est la Vie'. This was then played for the journalist – although it was evidently an early version, as we know the track was recorded again in London the following year and worked on further in 1976.

Key to understanding ELP in the post-*Brain Salad Surgery* period is Emerson's overriding passion to complete a classical piece he had been writing since 1973. Seemingly jaded by the electronic bombast of *Brain Salad Surgery*, he was keen to work with an orchestra and to create music that would earn the respect of his classical peers. He even said that when he listened back to earlier ELP albums, in his head he heard the sound of an orchestra augmenting the band.

Fortuitously, when the band got together to discuss their solo tracks, fully intending to release them independently, they discovered they had all been recording tracks using an orchestra. Greg Lake proposed the idea that instead of releasing three separate albums, they combine the tracks into a double album, giving themselves one side each and adding new band compositions on side four. Recording solo albums may have seemed a good idea in the immediate aftermath of *Brain Salad Surgery*, but the commercial reality was if they were all released at around the same time, sales would have collectively suffered. The decision to release a double album as a combined solo and band effort made sound financial sense. It would also appease Atlantic, who were beginning to call for a new ELP album. The name *Works* was suggested by Peter Sinfield who said, 'If you're going to be pretentious, you might as well do it big'.

Side one was entirely taken up by Emerson's classical piano composition, 'Piano Concerto No.1', with The London Philharmonic Orchestra conducted by John Mayer. Greg Lake's side contained five acoustic-based songs, which he'd worked on with Pete Sinfield. One of the tracks, 'C'est la Vie', was released as a single under just Lake's name. On side three, Carl Palmer presented an eclectic mix of rock, funk, classical and big band jazz. Arguably the least accessible side it nonetheless evidenced Palmer's broad musical taste and his dazzling drum and percussion skills.

Inevitably, it was side four that ELP's fans awaited most eagerly. It contained just two band tracks, 'Fanfare for the Common Man' and 'Pirates'. The former became ELP's biggest ever hit single, helping to propel *Works Volume 1* into the album charts. Despite this success, *Works Volume 1* received a mixed reaction from both hardcore fans and the music press. Since *Brain Salad Surgery* had been released, some three and a half years earlier, the music scene had undergone a dramatic change. In the UK in particular, bands such as ELP, Pink Floyd and Led Zeppelin were now dubbed 'dinosaurs', their mega-tours – which concentrated primarily on the lucrative US market – alienating fans who craved a simpler approach. Oblivious to the reasons behind the rise of punk rock, ELP – whose mantra had always been 'bigger is better' – were seen as outdated and out of touch almost overnight. The music press leapt on ELP's extravagances with glee, the band quickly becoming whipping boys. *Works Volume 1* was seen as the ultimate indulgence, the band satisfying their own egos at the expense of giving fans what they really wanted – which, if we're honest, was another *Brain Salad Surgery*.

With ELP looking to tour in support of the new album, Emerson's passion for orchestration turned to the live stage, 'I didn't want to go back on the road unless there was an orchestra. I wouldn't go with anything less. After three years, I didn't want to go back with the same set up, I needed a change – a new challenge'. He'd experimented playing live with an orchestra before, back in 1969, on The Nice's 'Five Bridges' – a piece commissioned as part of that year's Newcastle Arts Festival. Although the project was a success – 'Five Bridges' is very much the sound of a proto-ELP – Emerson was disappointed with the recording (from the Fairfield Hall in Croydon), saying that the orchestra's sound hadn't been fully captured due to limited use of microphones on stage. This time around, Emerson's plans were far more ambitious. With a burning desire to arrange some of ELP's older classics for the orchestra, playing them live alongside tracks from the new album – including his 'Piano Concerto No.1' – the band relocated in Montreal to rehearse with a hand-selected 70-piece orchestra. To achieve the best possible live sound, each musician was supplied with a state-of-the-art contact microphone. The orchestra alone required a team of six sound engineers. No expense was spared to give audiences the best possible sound of both band and orchestra.

The original plan was to tour North America in the Summer of 1977, taking the show to Europe later that year. One has to admire the courage of Emerson's conviction, as well as that of his band mates, who personally helped to fund the tour to the tune of one million dollars each. Those who experienced the gigs on the early dates of the US tour were bowled over by the sheer power and added dimension the orchestra gave to ELP's music. Emerson's brave decision had been vindicated in artistic terms but financially things were looking bleak. After three large shows were cancelled, the band's accountants announced the tour was now losing a frightening amount of money. To break even, attendance had to be close to 100% but they were only achieving around 80%. Touring with the 70-piece orchestra – who were all salaried – became a logistical and financial disaster. With immense reluctance, the band decided to pay off the orchestra and complete the North American tour as a three piece. The dates with an orchestra had lasted just over two weeks. The band and orchestra were later reunited for dates at New York's Madison Square Garden and Montreal's Olympic Stadium – the latter recorded for posterity on the *In Concert* live album. This was later released on CD as the extended *Works Live*. Footage of the Montreal concert was issued on videotape in the 1980s, as *Live '77*. It was reissued in 2002 as the double DVD set *Works Orchestral Tour / The Manticore Special*. The tour continued into 1978, extra dates helping the band recoup their costs. However, to the dismay of UK and European fans, no further dates were added after a Rhode Island gig on 13 March. It would be fourteen years before ELP played live again.

## Side one (Keith Emerson):

## 'Piano Concerto No.1' (Emerson)
  I.   First Movement: Allegro giojoso
  II.  Second Movement: Andante molto cantabile
  III. Third Movement: 'Toccata' con fuoco

Although Keith Emerson had not received any formal classical music training – aside from piano lessons when he was younger – it was no surprise when, in the wake of *Brain Salad Surgery,* he announced to his bandmates that he wanted to create his own classical music. The idea had been at the back of his mind since 1973, various piano pieces and musical ideas taking shape that he didn't want to be part of an ELP album. Gradually, the ideas were amalgamated into a concerto with three movements. The first, according to Emerson, had 'sort of a pastoral context', the second was 'sort of baroque', and the third was far more atonal and modern. Although undeniably classical in scope, Emerson was well aware of his formal composition limitations, saying, 'It may not have anything to do with 20th century music but it has a lot to do with me – and the way I write is unhindered by what is going on in today's music'. The meaning of the latter could be a reference to the rise of punk music at the time, virtuosity becoming decidedly uncool almost overnight. Or it could be Emerson commenting on the uncertainty of his classical credentials and whether such a weighty piece would be accepted.

There is little doubt that Emerson wished to be respected by his classical peers, possibly fuelled by the antipathy of music journalists towards ELP. He was frequently and very unfairly labelled a bluffer when it came to ELP's adaptation of classical music, so it was understandable he wanted to prove people wrong by creating something outside of the ELP sphere. He once said, 'I don't write for the music to be forgotten in six months. I like to think the music I've created is my own, that it hasn't come from anything else I've heard before. And it'd be nice for it to last.'

The concerto reflects his turbulent mood during the immediate post-*Brain Salad Surgery* area. After the last tour date in 1974, he settled into family life at his home in the heart of the East Sussex countryside. Both the first and second movements were written during this time, their reflective and pastoral nature reflecting his contentment. However, after his home was tragically destroyed by fire in April 1975 – although thankfully Emerson and his family were unscathed – most of his belongings, demo tapes and music manuscripts were lost. As a result, his mood became darker. He later admitted that the incident caused him to turn to drink and drugs. Suffering from depression, he went to live in the neighbouring county of Kent while his beloved house was restored. The third movement reflects this time.

'Piano Concerto No.1' was recorded in five sessions with the full 82-piece London Philharmonic Orchestra, during November and December 1975. Initially, Emerson sought the help of Jospeh Edger whom he'd worked with on *Five Bridges* during his time with The Nice. Although their previous collaboration had been successful, this time the pair didn't hit it off and Emerson was forced to look elsewhere for help in orchestrating his work. He eventually decided on John Mayer, who he'd been working with on another track, the altogether different 'Barrelhouse Shakedown'– which was eventually released on *Works Volume 2*. The Indian-born Mayer had been a violinist with the London Philharmonic Orchestra but had become better known for his compositional skills, fusing Indian music with Jazz, which is how he'd come to Emerson's attention.

The sessions with the London Philharmonic Orchestra were far from easy. Emerson was convinced that his non-classical status caused the musicians to look down at him and that they treated the sessions as a cash cow. In fact, initial recording sessions at Kingsway Hall, earlier in 1975, were considered unusable such was the apathy of certain parts of the orchestra. Relocating to De Lane Lea in Wembley, this time with a new, hand-picked brass section after Emerson's orchestrated parts were considered too difficult for the original musicians to play, Mayer and the ELP keyboardist achieved much better results. The same sessions also resulted in an orchestrated version of 'Abaddon's Bolero' and Scott Joplin's 'Maple Leaf Rag'.

Mayer's help and advice proved invaluable to Emerson, introducing him to new ideas in form, composition and orchestration. As a result, Emerson considered 'Piano Concerto No.1' his greatest compositional achievement. He was especially pleased when the BBC's classical radio station, Radio 3, played the entire piece twice. 'Piano Concerto No.1' eventually became part of *Works Volume 1* at Greg Lake's suggestion. Lake was greatly impressed with the piece, convincing Emerson to use it as his solo contribution to the double album. In retrospect, although it certainly gives the album gravitas, one does wonder whether Emerson would have achieved more respect from his classical peers if the piece had been released on a classical label instead – as was his original intention. Nevertheless, 'Piano Concerto No.1' is widely considered to be the best formally structured orchestral work ever composed by a rock musician.

When ELP toured North America in 1977 with the 70-piece orchestra conducted by Godfrey Salmon, 'Piano Concerto No.1' was abbreviated to the 1st and 3rd Movements. The full 20 minute-plus piece was, perhaps wisely, considered too long to fit into the band's set. Sadly, when the tour continued as a trio after the orchestra had been paid off, it disappeared from the set. Its final appearance at an ELP gig was at the Olympic Stadium in Montreal in August 1977. Although the entire gig was filmed and recorded, only the 3rd Movement appears on the resulting video (originally on the *Live '77* VHS, reissued on DVD as *Works Orchestral Tour*) and the album (*Works Live*).

**Side two** (Greg Lake):

**'Lend Your Love to Me Tonight'** (Lake, Sinfield)
**'C'est la Vie'** (Lake, Sinfield)
**'Hallowed Be Thy Name'** (Lake, Sinfield)
**'Nobody Loves You Like I Do'** (Lake, Sinfield)
**'Closer to Believing'** (Lake, Sinfield)
Echoing Emerson's desire to be regarded as a respected composer post-*Brain Salad Surgery*, Greg Lake began to gather together a set of songs for a solo album. He'd long suspected that his bandmates didn't totally value the contributions he had made to ELP's albums, a situation that became polarised

after 'Still... You Turn Me On' was vetoed a single. Weary after trying to complete with Emerson and Palmer's virtuosity, he seemed to re-evaluate his position, coming to the conclusion he was primarily a singer and not a guitarist or bass player. In fact, on *Brain Salad Surgery* it is noticeable that his bass playing was more restrained, so the feeling may have set in earlier. *Brain Salad Surgery* was also the last ELP album where Greg Lake was credited as being the sole producer.

In mid-1974, Lake was already saying he had an album's worth of material for a solo release, so in addition to the five songs that eventually made the cut for *Works Volume 1*, there must have been at least five more. 'Watching Over You' – which was eventually released on *Works Volume 2* – is presumably one. What the others are, remains unknown. Whether they later appeared on his 1980s solo albums, or on later ELP (or Emerson, Lake & Powell) releases is for conjecture – as is the tantalising possibility that demos of either unreleased songs or early versions of the *Works* tracks remain in the vault.

In the end, Lake chose five songs for inclusion on *Works Volume 1*, each one honed with the assistance of Pete Sinfield and with lush orchestration by Godfrey Salmon and Tony Harris. Who plays on Lake's tracks, and whether Emerson or Palmer contribute, has always been a mystery. The album credits give no clue as to who did what. Even Keith Emerson didn't know, seemingly hurt when the accordion part on 'C'est la Vie' was recorded by a session musician – despite him originally suggesting the idea to Lake. 'I think it was at a stage when we were being secretive about our solo projects. It was almost taboo for one of us to be in the studio when another of us was doing something for a solo album.'

Although undoubtedly finely-crafted and beautifully recorded, Lake's songs are a million miles away from the contemporary rock music ELP fans were used to hearing him sing and perform. Their arrangement was firmly in the vein of an AOR (adult oriented rock) singer songwriter, with Sinfield's lyrics steering clear of the sci-fi mysticism and clever wordplay he'd originally become renowned for in King Crimson. For many ELP fans, when they bought *Works Volume 1* when it was first released, it was all a bit of a shock and a disappointment.

Lake's first track – on side two of the original vinyl album – is 'Lend Your Love to Me Tonight'. It has a strong orchestral presence and an immaculate lead vocal – a feature of all of his songs on *Works Volume 1*. In terms of vocal performance, it is arguable whether he ever sounded better. A tale of passion, 'Lend Your Love to Me Tonight' was possibly one of a number of songs he wrote while on tour. Lake admitted, in a 1974 interview, he had a stockpile of suitable material for a possible solo album. 'I wrote them down all over the place, mainly while I was on tour of course, because we spent as much time on the road. I usually compose on guitar, though some things I did on piano,'

The second track, the aforementioned 'C'est la Vie', was recorded in Lake's favoured drop-D guitar tuning. In the US and the UK it was released as a single under Greg Lake's name, backed by ELP's 'Jeremy Bender' on the B-side – a bizarre choice. In France, 'C'est la Vie' was released under ELP's name backed by 'Hallowed Be Thy Name' on the B-side. Although unsuccessful as a single, it is probably the best known track on *Works Volume 1* aside from 'Fanfare for the Common Man'. 'C'est la Vie' was played live on the band's mammoth 1977-78 North American tour with the full backing of the orchestra and features on both the live video and *Works Live* from the iconic Montreal Olympic Stadium gig. When played live, the unknown session player's accordion part was replicated by Emerson.

Track three, 'Hallowed Be Thy Name' was written as far back as 1973. In fact, it was briefly considered for inclusion on *Brain Salad Surgery* losing out to 'Still... You Turn Me On'. One cannot help wonder how the track sounded back then, even as a demo, compared to its full orchestral treatment on *Works Volume 1*. The track features both Emerson and Palmer, the former contributing piano. He would later complain that his contribution was mixed so low in the mix that it was inaudible. 'Hallowed Be Thy Name' is also noteworthy for being the first time on an ELP track that Lake played harmonica. Sinfield's lyrics for 'Hallowed Be Thy Name' are more adventurous than for Lake's other *Works Volume 1* tracks, as indeed is the song's creative arrangement. One can easily imagine this being an ELP band performance, especially had the orchestration been replaced by Emerson's keyboards and if Palmer's drumming was less restrained.

'Nobody Loves You Like I Do', the fourth track, has a distinct Bob Dylan feel. Initially, the orchestration is kept to a minimum, allowing the song a chance to breathe. However, 'Nobody Loves You Like I Do', more than any other Greg Lake track on *Works Volume 1*, suffers from overproduction – the orchestra building in intensity and smothering the song as it reaches its climax. It would be interesting to hear this song in a rawer form, maybe as a pre-production demo, stripped of its lush production.

The final track on Lake's side is 'Closer to Believing'. Remarkably, the bare bones of the song were performed by Lake at an ELP gig in Germany in April 1973. Of all the songs that Lake contributed to *Works Volume 1*, this is by far the most cinematic. It reportedly took two years to complete to Lake's satisfaction. Stewart Young, ELP's manager, once flippantly said that he must have heard 'over fifty versions' before the final version. Again, this would have made an excellent ELP band track. Credit where due, however, the orchestration on 'Closer to Believing' is effectively atmospheric, building beautifully towards the finale, aided by a reverb-soaked choir.

Although Greg Lake's side on *Works Volume 1* is overproduced, the songs stifled by the orchestra rather than enhanced, the five tracks are beautifully sung and composed. They attempt to show Lake's wider influences and give him the chance to show his vocal talents rather than his virtuoso instrumental ability. For the diehard ELP fan in the 1970s, it was a musical dish probably too rich and diverse to be appreciated, but it benefits from a repeat listen today.

Emerson and Palmer's creative collaboration is sorely missed but the tracks give a clue as to what Lake's solo output would be like in the 1980s. Only 'C'est la Vie' was played live by ELP, which is a shame as it would have been great to hear any of these songs with a full band arrangement.

## Side three (Carl Palmer):

### 'The Enemy God Dances With The Black Spirits' (Prokofiev)
### 'LA Nights' (Palmer, Emerson)
### 'New Orleans' (Palmer)
### 'Two Part Invention in D Minor' (Bach, arranged Palmer)
### 'Food For Your Soul' (Palmer, South)
### 'Tank' (Emerson, Palmer)

Most ELP fans, on hearing the news that *Works Volume 1* contained a side by each of the band members, wondered what Carl Palmer had up his sleeve. Both Emerson and Lake's sides had songs and pieces in a style that, on the whole, fans expected. Palmer, on the other hand, despite his influence on ELP's music, was not known for his compositional skills. It was with some trepidation that fans dropped the needle onto side three when they first bought the record. To their surprise, the set of tracks that Palmer chose to include is probably the most progressive of all three sides.

An eclectic mix of progressive, classical, rock, funk and big band jazz, the surprise, in retrospect, is that side three omits Palmer's major piece of the time – his 'Percussion Concerto', composed by Joseph Horowitz with Palmer's assistance, that was recorded with the London Philharmonic Orchestra in the early months of 1976. This wouldn't see the light of day until it was released on Palmer's 2001 double CD, *Do Ya Wanna Play, Carl?* The band felt that including two classical concertos on *Works Volume 1* would have been too much for ELP's fanbase, so Palmer agreeing to leave it in the can for a future release. The decision probably cost Palmer's concerto the chance at gaining a wider audience – of which it is certainly worthy.

One can see the logic of leaving the 'Percussion Concerto' off *Works Volume 1*, but listening to the piece today one can't help but come to the conclusion that its inclusion would have benefited the album. As it was, Palmer decided instead to include some arguably less-essential tracks on *Works Volume 1*, some of which are perhaps musical sketches rather than fully realised pieces. That isn't to demean them, as Palmer's side is an enjoyable listen for progressive music fans who have broad horizons. More adventurous than Lake's set of songs, Palmer certainly did his credentials no harm whatsoever, especially on the opening track, Prokofiev's 'The Enemy God Dances with the Black Spirits'. If ever there was a classical track suitable for the ELP treatment, this was it. Here, Emerson and Lake's roles are replaced by the London Philharmonic Orchestra. Palmer later revealed that doing an ELP arrangement of the piece was actually discussed but he enjoyed the orchestral treatment so much he decided to include it. For those intrigued as to how a band treatment would have sounded, ELP played the piece live, as a trio, during the *Works* tour. The track appears on the double CD, *Works Live*.

The next track, 'LA Nights', couldn't be more different. Original titled 'LA '74', this funk rock work out features The Eagles' Joe Walsh on guitar and scat vocals, Emerson on piano and Moog, Lake's former King Crimson bandmate Ian McDonald on saxophone, with additional guitar by Snuff Walden. 'LA Nights' is a jam rather than a considered composition – Emerson gets a co-writing credit with Palmer – but is a welcome slice of rock fun on an album that is, for the most part, heavily weighed down by expectations and the serious nature of the music.

Track three, 'New Orleans', was written by Palmer with a view to recording it with The Meters, the renowned New Orleans-based funk band. Sadly, the session never took place. Instead, Palmer opted to go into the studio with Back Door, the UK jazz rock band who had opened some shows for ELP in 1974. Palmer also produced their *Activate* album, released in 1976. In a 1977 interview, Palmer said, 'I can compose things that could never fit in an ELP format and still get them out to the public. Like the track of mine off the new LP, 'New Orleans'. That's a very un-ELP sort of piece. I was about to record that with a group called The Meters – they come from New Orleans — but I couldn't get it together. The song still has that very New Orleans, dry, funky, empty sort of feel'. The track has a strong Joe Walsh vibe and features the kind of 'talkbox' style guitar typified on 'Rocky Mountain Way' – one of Walsh's best known tracks. Because Back Door are not credited on *Works Volume 1* and the fact they didn't have a guitarist – they were a trio consisting of only bass, drums and saxophone – it led to much speculation as to who played guitar on the track. Could it be Joe Walsh?

The period after *Brain Salad Surgery* saw Palmer take percussion lessons at the Royal Academy of Music in London from James Blades OBE. An accomplished percussionist, Blades famously played the gong that, for many years, introduced the Rank Organisation's films. He also provided the Morse code rhythm which the BBC used as a call sign during WWII. Palmer said in an interview with Modern Drummer magazine, 'I studied at the Royal Academy under James Blades for about 18 months. I was with Gilbert Webster from the Guild Hall for a further year. Most of the information obtained from these people was on classical percussion. I managed to apply quite a lot of this information into ELP.' Palmer's fourth track, Bach's 'Two Part Invention in D Minor', is thought to owe its inclusion on *Works Volume 1* as a thanks to Blades. It is a relatively straightforward run through, with a Harry South-arranged string arrangement over Palmer's vibes and with Blades himself on marimba.

The fifth track, 'Food for Your Soul' is unashamedly Palmer's tribute to his childhood drumming hero, Buddy Rich. Palmer said that he wanted to achieve a TV detective style soundtrack feel – which 'Food for Your Soul' achieves in some style. Although now sounding rather hackneyed to modern ears, big band jazz rock arrangements such as this were common during the 1970s. It certainly evokes the spirit of US TV shows of the era! The track is notable for two short Palmer drum breaks, which he executes with impressive discipline and restraint. Palmer produced 'Food for Your Soul' with Greg Lake. All other tracks on this side of the album were produced by Palmer alone.

The Buddy Rich influence extends to the closing track of side three, a reworking of 'Tank'. Played and arranged in the same style as 'Food for Your Soul' – the orchestration on both tracks was by Harry South. This new version of 'Tank' features Keith Emerson on piano, Moog and clavinet, largely revising his role on the original. Sensibly, Palmer chooses not to reprise his drum solo from the first album. In a live setting, however, on the *Works* tour, the solo was reintroduced. This can be heard on the band's *Works Live* CD album – although it didn't feature on the original *In Concert* LP.

Although Palmer's solo contribution to *Works Volume 1* is a mixed bag, it is, nonetheless, both exciting and creatively eclectic in a way that Lake's side two didn't manage to achieve. It definitely deserves reappraising. Whether many of the tracks deserve their place on an ELP album is another matter entirely. And, in a nutshell, that is the entire problem with *Works Volume 1*. It is too diverse for its own good and arguably too detached from the music that ELP had won a reputation for creating.

## Side four (ELP):

### 'Fanfare for the Common Man' (Copland, arranged by Emerson)

Undisputedly ELP's best known track and the band's only hit single, 'Fanfare for the Common Man' has it origins in a studio jam from 1976 when the band were at Mountain Recording Studios in Montreux, Switzerland. Greg Lake often told the story that the jam came about when Keith Emerson was playing around with Aaron Copland's composition on his then-new $50,000 Yamaha GX-1 synthesiser. After Lake joined in, playing a blues shuffle on his bass, accompanied by Palmer on drums, the piece suddenly came to life. The jam was recorded by sound engineer, John Tipperly, on a two track reel-to-reel tape machine. Although Lake claimed that the final version on *Works Volume 1* was the band's very first run through of the piece, that is doubtful. Lake said, 'We got a very live dirty R&B sound that was really incredible – and all done with one microphone. We hadn't played together for quite a while before that, apart from rehearsals and stuff. 'Fanfare for the Common Man' was thoroughly jammed, from top to bottom.' Although jamming is common for most bands when creating new material, it was unusual for ELP. Emerson preferred mapping each new piece out on manuscript before engaging with Lake and Palmer. Indeed, there is some evidence that 'Fanfare for the Common Man' was originally being worked out that way when Lake and Palmer first heard

Emerson playing it. Emerson said, 'It needed transposing, so I did that first. I wanted to improvise in a key that was sort of bluesy. It ended up in E. The rest of it was straightforward, really. You know, in order to get the shuffle sound, the timing had to be changed, but it was common sense.' This implies that the blues shuffle was Emerson's idea. Most likely the band jammed the track, trying out different ways of playing it, with the tape running not as a multitrack but just in stereo. Achieving a groove that met their approval they probably realised they couldn't better the feel of their jam, and used it as the basis for the final mix. The band then added overdubs, almost certainly including the intro that closely follows Copland's original composition. If ELP were to ever issue a deluxe *Works* set, it would be fascinating to hear these jams in their original raw, unedited state.

It is well known that Emerson was an admirer of Aaron Copland's work, so it is perhaps of little surprise that ELP would eventually tackle another of his compositions, particularly after the success of 'Hoedown' on *Trilogy*. To gain permission from the classical composer, Emerson sent him an edited mix. The response wasn't positive: Copland couldn't understand what the point of ELP's version was, as it more or less copied his original, adding nothing new. Emerson replied to Copland's publisher saying that he hadn't sent the full, unedited version, with the improvised section, because it might have offended him. To which the publisher said, 'Copland is like a twelve year old at heart, he'd love anything like that!' When Copland finally heard the full version, he granted permission saying, 'They're a gifted group. I allowed it to go because when they first play the Fanfare they play it fairly straight and when they end it, they play it fairly straight. What they do in the middle, I'm not sure how they connect that to my music, but they do it somehow I suppose.' When asked about ELP's improvised middle section and how it turned his original three minute composition into a nine minute track, Copland laughed. 'Exactly, well, it's those six minutes in the middle...!'

'Fanfare for the Common Man' is notable for its introduction of not only Emerson's Yamaha GX-1 but also Lake's new Alembic 8-string 'Scorpion' bass. Together, these two instruments formed the basis of a new sound – distinct to ELP and totally unlike any other band. The full polyphonic splendour of the GX-1, in Emerson's hands, is in many ways the sound of *Works* – especially the tour that was to follow, which also saw Lake take a small arsenal of Alembic guitars and basses with him. And, of course, Palmer was still relying on his iconic hand-engraved steel drum kit. ELP's new band sound on *Works Volume 1* divides fans to this day. Emerson's over-reliance on the GX-1, at the expense of his trusty Hammonds and Moogs, was something that sits less well with those who wanted the band to continue on the path they'd developed for *Brain Salad Surgery*.

There is also little doubt that *Works Volume 1* marked a change away from the earlier albums in terms of composition and approach, but it is food for thought as to whether the change would have been as marked, and therefore more palatable to hardcore fans, had Emerson also used his well-proven older instruments. What is undeniable, is that the new sound found favour with a wider audience – especially when 'Fanfare for the Common Man' was released as a single. To the surprise of many, possibly including the band themselves, it rose to number two in the UK singles charts in the Summer of 1977. It stayed in the UK top fifty for 14 weeks, only kept off the top spot by Hot Chocolate's 'So You Win Again'. The B-side was the track 'Brain Salad Surgery', at the time unreleased apart from its inclusion on the NME flexi disc promoting the album of the same name.

The video that helped promote the single was famously filmed at the Olympic Stadium in Montreal after a freak late Spring snowfall. The atmospheric footage captures the band miming to the full unedited album version, against the impressive backdrop of the empty white blanketed stadium. According to Lake, 'It was so cold that the promo had to be filmed in 30 second segments. We had to run into this trailer and dip our hands into hot water to stop them from freezing.' It was worth the effort, the resulting film becoming an instant ELP classic. In a heavily edited form it was showed on BBC's Top of the Pops chart show, helping to propel the single to number two.

Given the success of 'Fanfare for the Common Man' – which is the third best selling instrumental single in music history – it is little wonder it became a staple of ELP's live set, commonly played as an encore which segued into 'Rondo'. On very rare occasions, ELP played 'Fanfare for the Common Man' in its entirety, complete with the improvised middle section. The only known recording of the band playing the full version is on disc one of Volume Three of the *Original Bootleg Series*. All of the members of ELP went on to include 'Fanfare for the Common Man' in their live sets when they played in various post-ELP band projects.

It is probably true to say that ELP's version has become more widely played than Copland's original. It quickly became popular at sporting events and as the soundtrack for TV sports shows, especially in the USA. Its success as a single undoubtedly helped promote *Works Volume 1* – although what ELP's new fans thought of the rest of the tracks on the album is open to conjecture. Many fans believe that ELP's failure to capitalise on the success of 'Fanfare for the Common Man' was one of the reasons for their break up post-*Love Beach*. It is hard to disagree.

## 'Pirates' (Emerson, Lake, Sinfield)

This 13-minute-plus epic began life as a piece of music based on *Dogs of War*, the Frederick Forsyth novel about mercenary soldiers. Emerson had been approached to write a score for a movie based on the book, but the deal collapsed. He played the unused music to Lake, but the singer didn't like the theme. When Lake recruited Sinfield to help him with lyrics for the album, they suggested to Emerson that they revisit the music using pirates as the theme. Emerson liked the idea. 'The idea of pirates was good for my music. Because my music is very adventurous, much like an adventure novel, it demands to have visuals connected with it.' Apparently, Emerson's original idea was to use 'Pirates' as part of his intended solo album – although in what form it would have taken is unclear.

Lake said the reason he wasn't sure about using the mercenary theme is because he didn't think Emerson's music fitted. Instead, the composition reminded him of the sea – hence the 'Pirates' theme. 'We did a lot of research. Pete Sinfield and myself ordered all the books and films that had ever been written on pirates and we locked ourselves away for three weeks. We watched them all, and read all the books. And then we got started … the whole piece was written that way'. Sinfield later shed light more light on the process, 'The 'Pirates' theme was an allegory for a rock band on tour. When I read up on the subject it soon became obvious that pirates weren't at all romantic, they were reprehensible people – like the Kray Twins at sea! Keith's music was very Gilbert & Sullivan, it was extraordinarily difficult to get the true nature of piracy into it. I wrote most of it in Montreux, perhaps the least piratical place on Earth! I had to write to music that was already fixed and I only had 20 minutes to unfold this epic narrative. It should have been at least twice as long.'

There is little doubt that they did an excellent job, Emerson's music and Sinfield's lyrics fitting each other like a glove. The piece is colourful and dramatic, its storytelling compelling and cinematic. And despite Sinfield's concerns, it was concise. To the casual listener, the fact the music was composed in advance, before the lyrics and vocal melodies, is not at all apparent. The band started to record 'Pirates' at Montreux but eventually relocated to Paris to add the orchestration. According to Lake, 'It just so happened that opposite the studio was the Paris Opera House, and coincidentally Leonard Bernstein was conducting there at the time. Pete happened to know Leonard and he said he'd love Bernstein to come listen to 'Pirates' to see what he thinks. So, after an hour or two, across came Lenny. He sat down by me on the desk and he said, 'I hear you've got some music to play me.' I said, 'Yes, we've done this thing called 'Pirates' and I just think you might like to hear it.' I pressed the play button and he put his head in his hands. From beginning to end, he didn't move. And the piece ended, and now there's this moment of silence. You just don't know what's coming because Lenny wasn't backward in coming forward. If he didn't like something, you would be told. He looked at me and said, 'The singing's not bad'. And that's all he said! I'm sure he didn't realise that I was the singer.'

'Pirates' was orchestrated by John Mayer and recorded at Pathé Marconi Studios in Paris with the Orchestra de l'Opera de Paris, conducted by Godfrey Salmon. Emerson used his Yamaha GX-1 throughout, choosing sounds to contrast and blend with the orchestra's instruments. The rich palette of analog synthesiser sounds available on the GX-1 made it perfect for the job. Emerson described the GX-1 as a 'roadie's nightmare' because it was so fragile and heavy. He used the instrument on both *Works Volume 1* and *2, Love Beach* and *Emerson, Lake & Powell,* as well as his various soundtrack projects in the late-1970s and early-1980s. His first GX-1 was accidentally damaged at his East Sussex home when a tractor crashed into the barn that acted as his studio. Subsequently, he bought a GX-1 owned by Led Zeppelin's John Paul Jones – the actual instrument that was used on *In Through the Out Door* – cannibalising it to repair his damaged original.

For many ELP fans, although 'Pirates' was a welcome group effort after the indulgences on the solo sides, its lush orchestration was hard to swallow. With the loss of Emerson's Moogs and Hammonds and his enthusiastic use of the new GX-1, ELP now had a completely different sound. There's little denying that the orchestra on *Works Volume 1* adds drama and an added dimension but was it classic ELP? 'Pirates' is widely considered the band's last true epic but many fans prefer an altogether different version to the orchestrated track on *Works Volume 1.* After the band sadly parted with the 70-piece orchestra, only a couple weeks into their 1977 tour, 'Pirates' was retained in the set, played by them as a trio. Live recordings of this era demonstrate how effectively the three musicians tackle the ambitious arrangement. An excellent example is on disc 2 of the live compilation *A Time and a Place,* recorded at Memphis on 20 November 1977. 'Pirates' remained in ELP's set, sans-orchestra, when the band reformed in the early-90s – as heard on *Live at the Royal Albert Hall.* The track also appears on the DVD of the same name.

## *Works Volume 1* rarities and bonus tracks

1977 8-track
The 8-track issues of *Works Volume 1* – which are believed to have been released only in the USA and Canada – by necessity have an alternate running order to the original double vinyl album. This creates a completely different listening experience, solo efforts and band tracks running after each other. Emerson's 'Piano Concerto No.1' opens the album as per the vinyl but is then followed by all of Palmer's tracks bar 'New Orleans'. The first four of Lake's tracks are then followed by 'Fanfare for the Common Man', with Lake's fifth track, 'Closer to Believing', followed by Palmer's 'New Orleans'. 'Pirates' is then the final track as per the original album.

2001 UK Castle Music / Sanctuary Records edition
Serial number: CMDDD224
This issue is notable for three bonus tracks, recorded at the Indiana Hulman Center on 24 January 1978 – 'Tank', 'The Enemy God Dances with the Black Spirits' and 'Nutrocker'. It also comes with an informative 12-panel booklet.

2004 Sanctuary Midline edition
Serial number: SMDDD080
A reissue of the the 2001 edition.

2011 UK/Europe Legacy edition
Serial number: 88697848632
As per the Indiana bonus tracks editions but with a different style booklet.

2017 BMG deluxe edition
Serial number: BMGCAT2CD8
Remastered but no bonus tracks. New style of booklet with archive photo and band interviews.

# Works Volume 2  (1977)

Personnel:
Keith Emerson: synthesisers, piano, organ, accordion
Greg Lake: vocals, bass, acoustic guitar, electric guitar
Carl Palmer: drums, percussion
Released: November 1977
Highest chart place: 20 in UK, 37 US Billboard 200

Released at the end of 1977, *Works Volume 2* is a compilation of tracks from
various past recording sessions. Although widely derided as lacking focus
and 'a ragbag of leftovers' – as one review described it – many fans welcomed
the album's group tracks and the fact that it included notable rarities. *Works
Volume 2* reached no. 20 in the UK album charts and no. 37 in the USA – ELP's
lowest album chart placings at the time. Critical reviews were surprisingly
mixed, some reviews even praising the new release.

Crucially, *Works Volume 2* was released when the band were on tour in
North America, several songs finding their way into the band's set. Despite it
being a mixed selection of tracks, it hangs together pretty well as an album, the
shorter length of all songs – only two are over 4 minutes – making it an easy
listen. Only Greg Lake's 'I Believe in Father Christmas' jars slightly – as do all
Christmas songs when played out of season!

Emerson would later admit that the release of *Works Volume 2* was partly
to recoup some of the costs they'd lost while playing live with the 70-piece
orchestra. Its November release date, and the inclusion of Lake's Christmas
single – albeit with a different mix – was probably a cynical move to gain extra
sales over the festive period. Even the band portrait on the back cover had
a seasonal feel, depicting the band in the snow during their video shoot for
'Fanfare for the Common Man' at Montreal's Olympic Stadium.

Today, *Works Volume 2* is a curio. It is certainly not an essential release for
casual ELP fans but nonetheless contains several noteworthy tracks. Seven
of the eleven tracks on *Works Volume 2* had never been previously released.
Arguably, there wasn't a poor track on the album and it did much to highlight
ELP's more accessible less-symphonic side. Two of the tracks were brand new
recordings – side two's opener, 'So Far to Fall', and the album's closing track,
'Show Me the Way to Go Home'. The latter is one of the most unusual tracks
ever recorded by ELP, a well known standard and a very brave song to tackle.
It would close many of the band's live shows during the period. Interestingly,
Emerson once said that 'Fanfare for the Common Man' was not originally going
to be on *Works Volume 1*, with other band efforts destined to take its place.
Can we assume that these two tracks were among those earmarked to replace it?

## 'Tiger in a Spotlight' (Emerson, Lake, Palmer, Sinfield)

Recorded during the band's *Brain Salad Surgery* sessions in 1973, the
uptempo 'Tiger in a Spotlight' was planned for a single release in 1974 but

was cancelled. The track showcases Emerson's then-new Moog Constellation, although a German TV promotional slot, filmed after *Works Volume 2* was released, showing Emerson at his Yamaha GX-1. The footage, which can be seen on YouTube, is notable for a tiger that sits at Lake's feet while the band mime to a backing track – something that must have been uncomfortable for both the singer and the poor animal itself!

'Tiger in a Spotlight' was played by BBC radio DJ Alan Freeman on his Saturday Rock Show before the album was released, whetting fans' appetites. A long time supporter of the band, Freeman announced, 'The big ones are back' before giving it a spin. First impressions were positive but 'Tiger in a Spotlight' never found widespread favour among fans, despite the band choosing it to open their set on 1977's North American tour.

In a live setting, the track fared much better, no doubt as a result of it being played every night. An excellent version was recorded at ELP's iconic performance at the Olympic Stadium in Montreal in August 1977. This was included on the original live album of the gig, 1979's *In Concert* – later reissued as the expanded double CD live set, *Works Live*. Note that the 2017 CD reissue of *Works Volume 2* includes the entire *Works Live* set as bonus tracks. Another live version, recorded at the Indiana Hulman Civic Center on 24 January 1978, featured as a bonus track on the 2001, 2004 and 2011 CD re-issues of *Works Volume 2*.

## 'When the Apple Blossoms Bloom in the Windmills of Your Mind I'll Be Your Valentine' (Emerson, Lake, Palmer)

Another track from the *Brain Salad Surgery* sessions, 'When the Apple Blossoms Bloom in the Windmills of Your Mind I'll Be Your Valentine' has the distinction of having by far the longest ELP song title. Palmer's inclusion in the song credit is a clue that the track probably developed out of a studio jam. As with 'Tiger in a Spotlight' it doesn't sound fully developed – but in some ways it is all the better for it, free of any pretentions and overworking that sometimes marred their work. Lake's busy bass is almost searching for a definitive part, sandwiched between Palmer's busy drum groove and Emerson's vamped synths. Unusually for ELP, the track has a laidback feel, Emerson improvising Moog solos as it almost aimlessly careers to a finish. 'When the Apple Blossoms Bloom…' was never played live and possibly wouldn't have gained an official release in the vinyl era if not for *Works Volume 2*. One cannot help but wonder if any other similar jams are left unreleased in the ELP vault?

## 'Bullfrog' (Palmer, Aspery, Hodgkinson)

'Bullfrog' features Colin Hodgkinson on bass and Ron Aspery on saxophone and woodwind – both from the band Back Door. Their distinctive playing is immediately apparent to anyone familiar with their particular brand of jazz rock – as indeed it was on 'New Orleans' from *Works Volume 1*. An outtake from the same session as 'New Orleans', 'Bullfrog' has a lively Zappa-esque feel. Played at breakneck speed, with a touch of humour, it gives Palmer the chance to indulge himself using all manner of exotic sounds and rhythms. Progressive and left of centre, it is arguably superior to 'New Orleans', although cut from the same cloth.

A third track from the same sessions as 'Bullfrog' and 'New Orleans' – entitled 'The Pancha Suite' – was released on Palmer's 2001 anthology album, *Do Ya Wanna Play, Carl?* 'The Pancha Suite' was also issued in 2014 as a bonus cut on Victor's Japanese release of *Works Volume 2*, along with 'Bo Diddley' (an instrumental recorded in 1975) and 'Humbug' (the rather odd B-side of Lake's 'I Believe in Father Christmas' single).

### 'Brain Salad Surgery' (Emerson, Lake, Sinfield)

Recorded during the sessions for the *Brain Salad Surgery* album in 1973, the track of the same name first saw a release on a promotional flexi-disc that came free with the 3 November 1973 issue of New Musical Express. Intended to promote ELP's new *Brain Salad Surgery* album, it became something of a Holy Grail for ELP fans and collectors. Until the track was featured on the B-side of 'Fanfare for the Common Man', most fans were only familiar with it as a very low quality recording – an unfortunate side effect of flexi-discs. In the USA, the track was issued as a promo-only single backed by 'Still… You Turn Me On' – a release that was even more sought-after than the flexi-disc because so few were pressed.

When 'Tiger in a Spotlight' was mooted to be released as a single, the B-side was rumoured to be 'Brain Salad Surgery'. In hindsight, if Manticore had issued this back in 1973/74 – or indeed in 1977 – it could have performed well. It would certainly have made a decent follow-up to the 'Fanfare for the Common Man' single in the Summer of 1977. Why nothing was ever issued to take advantage of 'Fanfare for the Common Man's success is a mystery.

Like 'Tiger in a Spotlight', 'Brain Salad Surgery' features heavy use of Emerson's Moog Constellation. Although less simplistic, it has a similar loose feel and hints at Emerson's time in The Nice. Had ELP not decided on the orchestration route on *Works Volume 1*, who knows, tracks like these may well have pointed to an alternative future for the band. Unlike 'Tiger in a Spotlight', 'Brain Salad Surgery' was never played live.

### 'Barrelhouse Shake-Down' (Emerson)

Recorded at Advision Studios in 1975, 'Barrelhouse Shake-Down' features Emerson on piano, accompanied by a big band – arranged by Emerson and Alan Cohen. It was the B-side to Emerson's surprise 1976 hit single, 'Honky Tonk Train Blues'. A barrelhouse was an American drinking joint, typically a wooden shack where barrels of alcohol were stored. The kind of music played at these venues came to be known as 'barrelhouse', usually played on old out-of-tune pianos – a style and sound that Emerson emulates on this recording.

### 'Watching Over You' (Lake, Sinfield)

Although 'Watching Over You' is a leftover track from *Works Volume 1*, it benefits from a simpler production and arrangement. Lake said he wrote it as a lullaby for his daughter Natasha – although it was written retrospectively, when she was a young girl. On the track, Lake's acoustic guitar is backed by what sounds remarkably like a double-bass – or a very good simulation of such. Questions abound. Is this the only example of a double bass on an ELP track, and did Lake pay it himself? What we do know is that he played harmonica on 'Watching Over You', which Emerson emulated on his GX-1 when the track was played live. A live version from the New Haven Coliseum show on 30 November 1977 is included as a bonus track on the 2001, 2004 and 2011 CD re-issues of *Works Volume 2*. The song was also recorded for *Works Live*.

### 'So Far to Fall' (Emerson, Lake, Sinfield)

Opening side two, 'So Far to Fall', was originally held in reserve for inclusion on *Works Volume 1,* just in case 'Fanfare for the Common Man' was not approved by Aaron Copland. Emerson later admitted that even if Copland did give the thumbs up, Atlantic were keen to include 'So Far to Fall'. It was only after Emerson pleaded with Atlantic's Ahmet Ertegun that *Works Volume 1* should feature the full version of *Fanfare* that 'So Far to Fall' was left in the can.

Although rather over-embellished by a horn section, 'So Far to Fall' is something of a rarity in being a concise ELP track – despite it being the longest track on *Works Volume 2*!. The horns give the track a big band jazz feel, but played in the rock idiom. It is notable for being the only track on *Works Volume 1* and *2* that features Emerson on Hammond organ. Palmer's drumming is excellent throughout, although Lake's bass is rather low in the mix. Unusually, Lake sings in a pseudo American accent – his voice being previously renowned for its English quality. Interestingly, future solo and band releases would see Lake continue to sing in this way – yet another twist on ELP's changing sound post-*Brain Salad Surgery*.

### 'Maple Leaf Rag' (Scott Joplin)

Emerson had long been thinking of recording a solo album of piano pieces he had either written, or were in tribute to artists and composers he admired. This recording of 'Maple Leaf Rag' dates from late-1975 – from the same sessions as 'Piano Concerto No.1', with orchestration by John Mayer. Originally written by Scott Joplin in 1899, Emerson's take is rather rushed – although not nearly as fast as the lightning quick version he performs on *Works Live*. At just over two minutes long, it is the shortest track on *Works Volume 2*. Many have questioned its place on an ELP studio album. One can understand it being played live – for comedic or showmanship reasons – but the studio version adds little, if anything, to the original. One wonders what Emerson was trying to say by including it on *Works Volume 2*?

## 'I Believe in Father Christmas' (Lake, Sinfield)

By far the best known track on *Works Volume 2*, 'I Believe in Father Christmas' is something of a double edged sword. Because of the album's November release date, and because the track had been a number two hit single in the UK only two years earlier, one can imagine its inclusion was to help bolster sales over the festive season. Including it here with a different 'stripped back' mix was welcomed by ELP fans, helping to justify its place, but the question remains: who wants to hear a Christmas record all year round?

Lake frequently told the story of the song's genesis, 'I wrote it in my house in west London. I'd tuned the bottom string of my guitar from E down to D and got this cascading riff that you hear on the record. But I couldn't really place what the song was about. I was out driving one day and it was playing on my mind, and, all of a sudden, it occurred to me that the tune of 'Jingle Bells' fitted over it. And I thought …I wonder if this could be a song about Christmas?' Sinfield, who was charged with writing the lyrics, continued the story, 'Some of it was based on an actual thing in my life when I was eight years old, and came downstairs to see this wonderful Christmas tree that my mother had done. I was that little boy. Then it goes from there into a wider thing about how people are brainwashed into stuff. Then I thought, this is getting a bit depressing, I'd better have a hopeful, cheerful verse at the end. That's the bit where I sat down with Greg and we worked on it together. Then I twisted the whole thing with the last line, 'The Christmas we get, we deserve', which was a play on 'The government you get, you deserve'. I didn't necessarily explain all the politics or the thoughts behind it. It's not anti-religious. It's a humanist thing, I suppose. It's not an atheist Christmas song, as some have said.'

The track's distinctive instrumental motif, from Prokofiev's *Lieutenant Kijé* Suite, was added at Emerson's suggestion. Orchestration of the original single was by Godfrey Salmon. The track was recorded in November 1974, but it was decided not to quickly release it as a single as there wasn't enough time to promote it. Keeping their powder dry, Manticore issued it in time for Christmas 1975 – the song peaking at number two in the UK chart. Disappointingly, it only reached 95 in the USA. In fact, in the UK, it was only kept off the prestigious top slot on Christmas Day by Queen's 'Bohemian Rhapsody'. A promotional film in support of the single showed Lake surrounded by Bedouin tribesmen in the Sinai desert and outside the Qumran Caves in Israel that held the Dead Sea Scrolls. After Lake sings 'The Christmas we get, we deserve', footage of the Vietnam War flashes across the screen, reflecting the meaning of Sinfield's lyrics. The film ends with a young boy running to greet his father – a soldier returning home after war.

The version on *Works Volume 2* is identical in terms of Lake's vocals and guitar but isn't as heavily orchestrated and features both Emerson and Palmer. Two completely different versions were later issued as part of ELP's 1993 *The Return of the Manticore* box set, and on 2007's *From the Beginning* box set. The latter is an early version – thought to be a rough mix in preparation for the single. Lake also revised the track for the album, *A Classic Rock Christmas,* released in 2002. He played the song on his 2012 'Songs of a Lifetime' tour although it wasn't included on the album of the same name.

Many artists have covered 'I Believe in Father Christmas' and it remains a favourite on Christmas compilation albums. Without doubt it is Lake's most famous song, a fitting legacy to his ability as a songwriter, singer and musician.

## 'Close But Not Touching' (Palmer, South)

'Close But Not Touching' was recorded at around the same time as 'Food For Your Soul' and the re-worked 'Tank' on *Works Volume 1.* Its 1970s big band jazz styling by Harry South makes it a difficult listen – even an echo-laden guitar failing to lift the track from what is essentially a repeated horn riff that builds in intensity towards a crescendo. The best part is at the very end, when a lone flute plays over a synth drone, Palmer's drums subtly fading into the distance. 'Close But Not Touching' also appears on Palmer's 2001 anthology, *Do Ya Wanna Play Carl?* – strangely in preference to the superior 'Food For Your Soul'.

## 'Honky Tonk Train Blues' (Meade 'Lux' Lewis)

This influential early 'honky tonk' piece has been recorded by many artists since it was first written and recorded by Meade 'Lux' Lewis in 1927. Emerson had a hit single with it in 1976, basing his rendition on Bob Zurke's performance with the Bob Crosby Orchestra from 1938. The two recordings are almost identical, Emerson originally intending his version to be part of a solo album along with 'Barrelhouse Shake-Down' (the single's B-side). When Emerson finally released his first solo album in 1981, he named it *Honky,* featuring another Meade 'Lux' Lewis composition, 'Yancey Special'.

A promotional film in support of the 'Honky Tonk Train Blues' single was shown in 1976, on BBC's *Top of the Pops.* The film shows Emerson at an upright piano, in what looks to be a Twenties-styled nightclub, complete with potted palms. Smiling broadly, with sweat dripping off his nose as he vigorously bashes away at the piano, Emerson is accompanied by a horn section who look to be enjoying the moment as much as he did. It is well worth seeking out, as watching Emerson enthusiastically play this fast-paced piano instrumental gives the track extra excitement, totally vindicating its inclusion on *Works Volume 2.*

## 'Show Me the Way to Go Home' (Irving King)

Orchestrated by Emerson and Godfrey Salmon and recorded at the same Paris sessions as *Works Volume 1's* 'Pirates', this well known song from the 'Great American Songbook' is a surprising number for ELP to tackle. To the band's credit, they play it in a supremely mature fashion that always surprises their detractors. Throughout, Lake puts in a strong vocal performance, with Emerson playing assured Art Tatum-style piano. The entire track is impressively restrained, allowing the orchestra, conducted by Salmon, to swing behind Palmer's tight drumming.

Played live during their 1977 and 1978 North American tours, 'Show Me the Way to Go Home' became the band's final wave goodbye to audiences after the encores of 'Fanfare for the Common Man' and 'Rondo'. It was captured live at ELP's iconic Olympic Stadium gig in Montreal in August 1977 on *Works Live* (which was included as part of the 2017 CD reissue of *Works Volume 2*) as well as on the *Live '77* video (later released on DVD as *Works Orchestral Tour*). Another live version, which was recorded at the Indiana Hulman Centre on 24 January 1978, features as a live bonus track on the 2001, 2004 and 2011 CD re-issues of *Works Volume 2*. A slightly later and looser performance, albeit an audience bootleg recording from a 1978 Chicago gig, is on Volume Four of the *Original Bootleg Series.*

## *Works Volume 2* rarities and bonus tracks

2001 UK Castle Music / Sanctuary Records edition
Serial number: CMRCD225
This issue is notable for three bonus live tracks – 'Tiger in a Spotlight' and 'Watching Over You' from the New Haven Coliseum show on 30 November 1977 and 'Show Me the Way to Go Home' from the Indiana Hulman Centre on 24 January 1978.

2004 Sanctuary Midline edition
Serial number: SMRCD081
A reissue of the the 2001 edition.

2011 UK & Europe Legacy edition
Serial number: 88697848642
As per the Indiana bonus tracks editions but with a different style booklet.

2017 BMG deluxe edition
Serial number: BMGCAT2CD9
Remastered with the complete *Works Live* album as bonus tracks.

# Love Beach (1978)

Personnel:
Keith Emerson: synthesisers, piano, organ, accordion
Greg Lake: vocals, bass, acoustic guitar, electric guitar, guitar synthesiser
Carl Palmer: drums, percussion
Released: 10 November 1978
Recorded: Compass Point Studios, Nassau, Bahamas
Highest chart place: 48 in UK, 55 US Billboard 200

Although fans welcomed the return of ELP, free of the orchestration on *Works Volumes 1* and *2*, *Love Beach*, without any question whatsoever, is the band's most controversial album. Recorded in 1978, at Compass Point Studios in the Bahamas – close to Emerson's Nassau home – the *Love Beach* sessions did not go as smoothly as they'd hoped. According to Keith Emerson, both Lake and Palmer really disliked being on Nassau and desperately wanted to get the recording done as quickly as possible. For tax reasons, Lake actually bought a house on the island for the duration of his stay, whilst Palmer rented a hacienda. The entire writing and recording process took over four months to complete.

With very little evidence of collaborative group writing, *Love Beach* is an album of two halves. It is of two halves – part-progressive and part-AOR. Side one was mostly written by Lake and Sinfield and consists of shorter tracks. Side two is one epic track, primarily written and arranged by Emerson. Lake and Palmer left the island before mixing of the album was finished, leaving Emerson to complete the task. With Lake resigning his traditional ELP production duties, a role he'd had until *Brain Salad Surgery*, it is poignant to note that nobody is credited as producer on the album's sleeve notes.

ELP's cause wasn't helped by the album sleeve, which shows them looking for all the world like the Bee Gees. *Love Beach* has gone down in rock music history as being one of the worst album covers ever. For a band who had only released *Brain Salad Surgery* – one of the best-ever album designs – only a few years previously, it was all a massive shock for fans. To early buyers, eager to place a brand new ELP album on their decks, the cover and title alone should have been enough for them to expect the worst. Even the merchandising insert raised eyebrows – selling embroidered satin tour jackets and jogging shorts! For ELP, it looked as if year-zero of punk had never happened. Punk's angry diatribes aimed at aloof rock stars like ELP and Led Zeppelin living in their ivory towers seemed unerringly accurate. It was suddenly a complete embarrassment to be an ELP fan – more so than it ever had been before.

To help understand *Love Beach*, we need to look at the background behind the making of the album. It is widely considered to have been recorded as the result of a contractual obligation to Atlantic Records. None of the band were interested. Atlantic President, Ahmet Ertegun, was calling the shots and it was his idea to call the album *Love Beach*. Emerson absolutely detested the title, even going as far as conducting a poll at O'Hare Airport in Chicago to gain public opinion. The result was overwhelming – nobody who was polled thought *Love Beach* was a suitable title for an ELP album. But Ertegun wouldn't budge, telling the band that the title made no difference. Emerson countered by saying, 'It makes a difference to me because it doesn't fit the image of the band'. Sadly, Ertegun and Atlantic had already made their mind up, *Love Beach* was going to be the album's title.

Atlantic were further adamant that ELP deliver a commercial album. Their misunderstanding of ELP's fanbase was almost total, thinking that the commercial success of 'Fanfare for the Common Man' could be built upon by the band delivering a set of shorter AOR-based songs, bolstered by a couple of more typical ELP tracks. Emerson had no interest in the former, Lake had little interest in the latter. In hindsight it is easy to say that they could have buried their differences to help protect the valuable ELP brand they had developed, but they were exhausted after the overlong *Works* tour and tired of being exiled from the UK – thanks to the British Government's rigid tax laws at the time. At the end of the *Works* tour Emerson said, 'We were considering a final separation. It was at the back of all our minds. The orchestra tour plagued Greg and Carl as both a financial and artistic disaster. A view I totally disagreed with. One thing was certain, in order to continue we would have to do a lot of cutting down. We even discussed a piano, bass, drums format'. From a fans point of view, it is a shame they didn't pursue this idea, maybe also allowing Emerson to play his Hammond! The fans would have loved that kind of approach.

When you add into the mix the massive sea change the music industry had undergone since ELP's mid-70s heyday – something that record companies were still, at the time, struggling to come to terms with – it easy to see why the band had become 'dinosaurs'. Emerson was right, the smart move would have been to lie low and take stock but Atlantic wanted their pound of flesh and were pushing hard for a new album. Had ELP failed to deliver, all three would have been liable to a substantial financial penalty that probably would have bankrupted them.

No tracks off *Love Beach* were ever played live by the band although Palmer would later play 'Canario' with his own trio. He admitted, 'We actually decided to split around the time of *Love Beach*. I tried to organise a farewell tour and spent two months working on it... it was coming along well. Then there were internal problems within the band... and I realised we should just stop. You only have so much energy in life.' The split was finally announced at the end of 1979. Music press articles said that all three members were already involved with solo projects – Palmer with 1PM, Emerson creating film scores, and Lake writing a solo album. Thankfully, we now know that ELP didn't spilt forever – they'd triumphantly return in the early-90s. *Love Beach* may have been their worst album but it wasn't their last.

**'All I Want is You'** (Lake, Sinfield)
**'Love Beach'** (Lake, Sinfield)
**'Taste of My Love'** (Lake, Sinfield)

These guitar-orientated tracks from side one of *Love Beach* were written by Lake, with lyrics by Sinfield. Emerson and Palmer's input was minimal. Lake's guitar is far more dominant here than on any other ELP album – Emerson's keyboards reduced to inconsequential fills and unimaginative backing. The sound of Emerson's Yamaha GX-1 and two new additions to his keyboard arsenal – Korg 3100 and 3300 polyphonic synths – pervade all tracks on *Love Beach*, but seem less colourful and creative than on *Works Volume 1*. Palmer's role is restricted to that of a session musician, although his simpler and more economic drumming fits the tracks well – something he would later develop with Asia. It is also worth noting that he was now playing a classic wooden Gretsch kit, his huge stainless steel kit having recently been retired (eventually to be bought by Ringo Starr).

'All I Want is You', the album's lead track, was released as a single. The band even appeared on BBC's *Top of the Pops* to promote it. In the footage, as the band mime to a backing track, Emerson is seen fiddling with the settings of his GX-1, whilst Lake plays a Roland GS-500 guitar synthesiser. The sound of this guitar synth is quite prominent on *Love Beach*, especially on Lake's songs. At times it is difficult to discern whether the synth sounds we hear are being made Lake or by Emerson.

The album's title track, 'Love Beach', is named after the shoreline opposite Compass Studios, where the band were recording. Although one of the better songs on the album, it is not in any shape or form an ELP track. It sounds exactly what it is – a Greg Lake composition with Emerson as a largely indifferent session man. Lake actually turns in a decent vocal performance, despite the song's totally insipid lyrics – Sinfield seemingly showing as much disinterest in the project as ELP themselves. To be fair to Palmer, his drumming is lively throughout and he impressively locks in with Lake's bass to provide an almost jaunty backing. Not that I'm sure 'jaunty' is what the 'Love Beach' theme required!

The lyrics for the third track, 'A Taste of My Love', are so full of immature sexual innuendo that one can only imagine Sinfield and the band were having a joke at the record company's expense. Perhaps they were hoping the song would be banned to create some much-needed controversy? Musically it fares little better. Full of nautical synth motifs, similar to those on 'Pirates' and Emerson's 1981 solo album, *Honky*, we're left wondering what the link between the lyrics and music actually is. Maybe with different lyrics and an Emerson solo, 'A Taste of My Love', could have been improved – an impression bolstered by listening to 2001's Sanctuary Records edition of the album, which includes a band rehearsal of the track. This makes absolutely fascinating listening and gives a startling glimpse as to how the *Love Beach* tracks could have sounded with beefier production. Interestingly, the track has no bass guitar whatsoever, Lake playing his Roland GS-500 guitar synthesiser instead. All low end duties are covered by Emerson's GX-1. On the album's 2017 deluxe reissue, the excellent rehearsal track has inexplicably been dropped, replaced by a new set of bonus tracks, one of which is a 'Taste of My Love' remix. Although a definite nudge in the right direction, the song now sounding far more upfront, it isn't a patch on the raw rehearsal. In this autor's opinion, that was the way to go!

Those wanting to understand how it all went so badly wrong for ELP need to hear all of the rehearsals included as bonus tracks on the 2001 and 2017 reissues of the album. They shed invaluable light on what could have been, had ELP taken a more boisterous tack.

### 'The Gambler' (Emerson, Lake, Sinfield)

It isn't too much of a stretch to imagine 'The Gambler' on *Works Volume 1,* or even on an earlier ELP album. And Emerson is actually given a solo! It is the only track on *Love Beach* co-written by Emerson and Lake. Sinfield is again responsible for the lyrics, which are an improvement to those on 'A Taste of My Love' but lack panche. We're left wondering why Sinfield was employed on *Love Beach* as his lyrics seem to detract rather than enhance the songs. To be fair, he has never defended his contribution, instead taking a rather mercenary stance. Were Lake's lyrics on earlier ELP albums really that bad he needed help? The evidence seems to indicate otherwise.

### 'For You' (Lake, Sinfield)

Aside from the rather clumsy intro, 'For You' is arguably the most successful song on side one. Heavily infused with Lake's GS-500 guitar synth and backed by some inspired keyboard touches from Emerson, the track has a definite ELP feel. Although primarily a Lake solo composition, Emerson's flourishes echo the work the two would achieve on the *Emerson, Lake & Powell* album. It is almost a shame when the track begins to fade, as you feel it is just about to shift up a gear and take off, with Emerson taking an elongated solo!

### 'Canario' (Rodrigo-Vidre)

'Canario' is based on the fourth movement of Spanish composer Joaquín Rodrigo's *Fantasía Para un Gentilhombre.* Composed for guitar and orchestra in 1954, it was written for Andrés Segovia – the 'gentilhombre' referred to in the title. The only classical adaptation on the album, it is most ELP fans' favourite *Love Beach* track.

Emerson once said of *Love Beach*, 'I think some of it stands up fairly well. On the other hand there's no way it could be called classic ELP. I feel there was a certain charm in 'Canario'. It had almost the same effect as 'Hoedown' or something'. Listening to 'Canario' today, you can see Emerson's point but it falls far short of the intensity they achieved with 'Hoedown'. Part of that can be put down to the GX-1's distinctive sound, which hasn't dated well. However, at around the two and half minute mark, the track starts to take off, with Emerson improvising furiously, his GX-1 sounding far less polite. It is a shame this section ends too soon, and you get the feeling the band realised they were straying into non-commercial territory, something Atlantic may have been averse to.

It would have been great to hear ELP play this track live, ideally with Emerson on his trusty Hammond as opposed to the GX-1. A bonus track on both 2017's remastered CD of *Love Beach* and 2001's Sanctuary issue features 'Canario' in rehearsal. As with the 'A Taste of My Love' rehearsal, you want to shout, 'This is more like it!' Palmer is evidently enjoying himself here, so little wonder he chose to perform this track with his trio – the only *Love Beach* track ever to be performed live. Palmer's version can be heard on his 2002 CD, *Working Live, Volume 1*.

### 'Memoirs of an Officer and a Gentleman' (Emerson, Sinfield)

The Emerson & Sinfield songwriting credit is unique on an ELP album and it tells us much about how the piece was written. It is the sole 'epic' track on *Love Beach* and was, for the most part, well-received. ELP fans were happy that the band had included at least one long track on the album, taking solace in its ambitious instrumentation. Sinfield had been asked by ELP's manager, Stewart Young, to help the band out. We can only presume that such was Lake's apathy, Young was hedging his bets by recruiting the seasoned lyricist. Sinfield agreed to come out to Nassau, but only if he could work alone. He was aware of the simmering tensions within ELP and thought that he could more easily deliver lyrics if he wasn't dragged into any inter-band politics. He arrived at Nassau with his girlfriend, thinking that if nothing else they could have three pleasant weeks in the sun!

His lyrics for 'Memoirs of an Officer and a Gentleman' were delivered to the band in stages. He'd write one part, deliver it for them to work on, then go back and work on some more words. The story he chose to tell to accompany Emerson's music is of a young British army officer. This obviously privileged chap goes through public school, then to officer training at Sandhurst. He meets and marries the girl of his dreams before being sent to war. By the reference to 1938, we know this is World War Two – although the lyrics are so twee in places, it wouldn't be out of place set in World War One. The last part is told via letters he sent back to his wife from the front. In a twist at the end, it isn't the young officer who is killed, but his wife, presumably in an air-raid. Emerson later said that he was unhappy with the banality of some of Sinfield's lyrics. In Emerson's own words, 'The lyrics are a bit gross, but it was because everybody but me wanted to get the hell out of Nassau'.

What is strange about 'Memoirs of an Officer and a Gentleman' is that the entire 20-minute track has something of a demo feel to it. Lake later admitted that the theme wasn't something that inspired him greatly, 'We did the best we could, but we didn't really have much belief in the project'. The rather one dimensional subject matter seems more at home in a TV drama than on the concept album of a progressive rock band. Compare and contrast, for example, to how a broadly similar theme of loss and war was dealt with by Roger Waters and Pink Floyd on their altogether much darker *Final Cut* album. ELP's treatment is almost like a musical, lacking any gravitas. Perhaps, had another subject have been chosen to marry up to Emerson's music, it could have been very different. As it stands, it all sounds gratuitous and lightweight.

That said, it is fantastic to hear Emerson be given the chance to stretch out across all four movements. You can almost hear him willing the band to give 'Memoirs of an Officer and a Gentleman' their best shot. This is especially apparent on the intriguing rehearsal snippets included as bonus tracks on both the album's 2017 reissue and the earlier 2001 Sanctuary release. All are well worth hearing. It is also notable that in the rehearsals the band sound as if they're having fun, which is in direct contrast to their later reports about wanting to get away from Nassau as soon as possible. What changed I wonder?

## *Love Beach* rarities and bonus tracks

2001 UK Castle Music / Sanctuary records edition
Serial number: CMRCD226
This issue is notable for three bonus tracks – band rehearsals before recording took place – 'Canario', 'Taste of My Love' and 'Letters from the Front'. It also comes with an informative 12-panel booklet.

2004 Sanctuary Midline edition
Serial number: SMRCD079
A reissue of the the 2001 edition.

2011 UK & Europe Legacy edition
Serial number: 88697848662
Remastered with bonus tracks identical to the 2001 and 2004 reissues.

2017 BMG deluxe edition
Serial number: BMGCATCD10
Remastered plus '1978 Alternate Mixes' of the whole album, plus three bonus 1978 rehearsal out-takes – 'Canario', 'Letters from the Front' and 'Prologue / The Education of a Gentleman'. Note that 'Canario' is only 2:23 minutes long here, compared to 4:39 on the earlier reissues. It isn't clear whether this has been cleverly edited from different takes or is a different version. Both versions are almost identical up until 2:20. 'Letters from the Front' on the earlier reissues is 8:53 minutes long, whereas on this issue it is only 4:01. Again, it is unclear whether it is a different take or an edited remixed version. All of the rehearsal out-takes on the reissues are worth hearing – providing a fascinating insight to the writing of the *Love Beach* material. And despite all members

of ELP saying that the *Love Beach* sessions were fraught, from the sound of laughter and banter on these out-takes, it sounds as if they were having fun! Best of all are the '1978 Alternate Mixes'. They shed new light on all of the *Love Beach* tracks, improving them greatly. This is recommended listing for every ELP fan. Lastly, also included with this 2017 edition is a new style of booklet complete with a tribute to Keith Emerson and Greg Lake who had both passed away by the time the CD was released.

# Black Moon (1992)

Personnel:
Keith Emerson: Korg and Yamaha synthesisers, Hammond organ, Steinway grand piano
Greg Lake: vocals, bass & guitars
Carl Palmer: drums & percussion.
Relcased: 27 June 1992
Recorded: Marcus Studios, Front Page Recorders, mixed at Conway Studios
Producer: Mark Mancina
Engineer: Steve Kemper
Highest chart place: 78 US Billboard 200

When ELP reformed in 1991, their new album, *Black Moon*, took major cues from *Emerson, Lake & Powell*. However, Lake later admitted, 'Cozy was great. When he joined the band, it was very, very nice ... a great player, and a lovely guy. But the strange thing was, it wasn't ELP anymore. The chemistry was different. There's something that Carl brought to the band which made ELP.' The story always told is that Palmer was still busy with Asia when Emerson and Lake felt the time was right to try again, so they were forced to recruit a different drummer. Although Palmer gave his blessing, it turns out he was a bit aggrieved at being left out. 'The way I looked at it, they were promoting my back catalogue ... but I thought it was a little petty that they couldn't wait'. Lake would often discuss of the magic of ELP's chemistry, so it was inevitable that Palmer's presence was missed. As Lake added, 'Carl Palmer is very effervescent. Carl's personality was so energetic, and ELP missed that ingredient.'

After the Emerson, Lake and Powell project ended – allegedly because they'd spent their entire budget on the first album and its accompanying tour, leaving nothing for a second album – Emerson busied himself with a solo project. Working with Kevin Gilbert, the American multi-instrumentalist, singer and composer, he began to put together an album of ELP-flavoured material, toughened by the addition of hard rock guitar and straight-ahead drumming. It could, and should, have provided a platform for greater things to come. Fate, however, intervened and before the album was completed the project was shelved. It remained unreleased until 1995.

The reason for the hiatus, was a call from Phil Carson to Emerson suggesting that ELP reform as 'flagship' band for his new record label, Victory Records. Emerson called Lake and Palmer and they agreed to meet up – and as is the way of musicians, they got together for a jam. According to Palmer, as they played though 'Tarkus', the old magic immediately returned. A story was spun that Carson had approached Emerson to write a movie soundtrack, with the fictitious name 'Black Crow' – or according to some sources, 'Black Chrome'. Emerson supposedly then asked his old bandmates to help out. However, it was all a PR smokescreen in case word got out that ELP had reformed – possibly because Palmer was still in Asia at the time.

Enthused at the possibilities of a reunion, Emerson said, 'It's quite amazing. I feel optimistic about it because we have all our old friends around us. I've always felt nervous about working with other people. You don't know how they're going to react or behave. Being with ELP is like having the family back again'. With Palmer having extricated himself from Asia, the band began to prepare a set of songs for recording. Three tracks from Emerson's solo project were chosen, although all were renamed, for reasons unknown. Crucially, the band began to write together for the first time in years. As with *Love Beach*, Lake stepped aside from production duties. Emerson always said that Lake had never actually been asked by the band to produce their albums, it was just something he gravitated to. Emerson and Palmer initially shrugged off his place at the mixing desk, reasoning that Lake's experience in helping to produce King Crimson's debut album would stand them in good stead on their debut. They were wise to do so, as his production on early ELP albums is a vital ingredient in their classic sound.

Under the tensions surrounding the making of *Works Volume 1*, Lake's bandmates questioned his production role, which led to a lingering resentment. Possibly as a result of this, one of Carson's stipulations was that an external producer be brought in 'to lighten the load on Lake'. Emerson commented on the situation, 'Now we work together and a lot of the strain has been taken out by having a producer. In the past we each took too much responsibility and it just wore us down. In the autumn of our years we have become more forgiving, which is a very important quality'.

The producer chosen was the then-relatively unknown Mark Mancina. He would later become one of Hollywood's best known and most successful composers and arrangers. The brief given to Mancina was to galvanise all three musicians to create a cohesive 'modern' ELP album. Wary of going down a similar commercial route to *Love Beach*, the band knew they were treading on difficult ground. Yet they also knew that for the reunion to be a success they had to update their sound. In addition to Mancina, the production team also included Ian Morrow and John Van Tongeren, who brought in a wealth of studio programming expertise – a huge factor in the making of *Black Moon*.

When *Black Moon* was released in June 1992, it generally gained positive reviews. However, there were the inevitable scathing comments from some music journalists – ELP being a easy target for any lazy hack with an axe to grind. Although it would be ridiculous to claim *Black Moon* is on a par with the band's classic albums, from beginning to end it contains a very listenable set of mature prog-tinged tracks in the AOR vein. The album retains ELP's distinct sound, but thanks to Mancina, it adds a contemporary sheen. Today, *Black Moon* divides opinion among ELP fans – some 'keyboard warriors' suggesting it isn't as good as *Love Beach*. Nevertheless, although *Black Moon* isn't their best album, at the time it was great to have them back. The band sound older and wiser, and under Mancina's direction they play it very safe, but *Black Moon* is also a true band effort. That was wonderful to hear after years of lukewarm solo efforts – some of which masqueraded as ELP albums!

The icing on the cake, especially for ELP fans in the UK, was when the band toured in support of the album. For the first time since 1974, ELP played UK gigs, including a clutch of dates at London's prestigious Royal Albert Hall – a venue that had previously banned Emerson due to his burning of the Stars and Stripes at a Nice gig! The tour opened in the USA on 22 June 1992. After gigs in Japan in September, the band finally arrived in Europe, playing in Verona on 26 September. The much-anticipated Royal Albert Hall dates were on 2 and 3 October – with a third date added later that month. ELP stayed on the road well into the following year, on a world tour that finally ended in Buenos Aires on 5 April 1993.

## 'Black Moon' (Emerson, Lake, Palmer)

'Black Moon' became the lead single off the album, Victory Records having enough faith in the song to invest in a slick video, showing the band 'playing' in an Italian marble quarry. Although not a hit, the video gained limited rotation on MTV, the shoot gaining the band valuable coverage in the mainstream press – including an article in a glossy weekend newspaper supplement in the UK.

With Lake once more penning his own lyrics, on 'Black Moon' he tackles a theme far from the rather insipid words Sinfield had created for *Love Beach*. According to Lake, much of the album was written against the background of the Gulf War. He felt compelled to write the lyrics after watching the dramatic news footage of oil wells burning in the desert. His words, 'We never learn, even deserts burn' sums up the mood many of us felt at the time. He later added, 'I saw this report about all these oil wells being set alight and this picture had the sun blacked out by all this smoke, but you could still see it and it looked like the moon... that started me thinking'.

The music for 'Black Moon' has its origins in a piece Emerson had been playing around with. At a band rehearsal one day, 'I went out for lunch and when I came back, Greg and Carl were hammering out a heavy rock thing. Without saying a word, I went to the keyboard and struck this chord'. Immediately, it was turned into something more substantial using the music he'd been playing around with. He admits he had to try hard to keep it simple, 'There are lots of times I had to be held back from doing too much'. He also confessed he was uneasy at making the entire track too rocky: 'I wasn't satisfied at the idea of ending with a heavy head-banging piece ... the ending took a lot of crafting'.

It was worth the effort as 'Black Moon' became a standard bearer for the entire album. First impressions for ELP fans were very favourable – it seemed as if Mancina had managed the impossible, by bottling ELP's core sound into a relatively short commercial track. However, it still needed editing for release as a single – down from the seven minute album version to just under five minutes. Both versions can be heard on the album's 2017 reissue. Note the single has a different and much shorter intro!

### 'Paper Blood' (Emerson, Lake, Palmer)

Another band composition, this time featuring Lake on harmonica – a repeating trait on later ELP albums. Uptempo and hard-hitting, one can almost imagine Mancina encouraging the band to rein in their enthusiastic tendencies to overplay! The lyrics deal with the fact that it is all too easy to forget the things that matter in life and to get corrupted by money. Lake recalls that one day while he was driving in London, 'I stopped at traffic lights and on the right hand side of me was a chauffeur-driven car with just a dog in the front passenger seat while on to the left was a tramp fishing for stuff out of the dustbin, looking for food.' He says he couldn't shake the image, 'This ridiculous sight stuck with me for days and I thought, what is that about? And the answer is money, the lack of it and too much of it. Then I thought it's like blood, money is like blood, paper blood. That was the catalyst for the song'.

For Emerson, 'Paper Blood' was, 'A great opportunity to rip hell out of the Hammond. The truth is, I was never completely happy with the sound I used to get in the '70s but on this album, I think I've finally achieved the ultimate Hammond sound'. ELP fans may well take issue with that, as whilst it is always welcome to hear Emerson attack his Hammond, on *Black Moon* it is far weaker and 'fizzier' than the aggressive sound on earlier ELP albums. To many, that earlier Hammond sound is very much what ELP were about.

One wonders whether the theme of 'Paper Blood' is one of the reasons behind the album's cover illustration. Could the merry-go-round (or carousel in the US) be a visual metaphor for life? Perhaps it is out of control, with the dollar bills spinning frivolously away. The cover for *Black Moon* has always been something of a mystery. Do the paintings on the canopy hint at some of the themes Lake tackles? One of them seems to be an illustration of a lake – or is it the blue lagoon in the lyrics to 'Black Moon'? It is like an unsolved Dan Brown mystery, complete, if you look closely, with mystical symbols!

### 'Affairs of the Heart' (Lake, Downes)

The second single off the album, 'Affairs of the Heart', was written by Lake with Geoff Downes, the Asia and Yes keyboard player. It was originally part of their joint Ride The Tiger project. Lake remembered the idea for the song came when he was on holiday in Venice, 'There is a hotel there called the Danieli. In the lobby is this huge and beautiful chandelier and there was this beautiful girl sitting across the other side ... the whole opening of the song just wrote itself, there and then'. When Lake played Emerson the version he'd recorded with Downes, it was suggested they do an acoustic version instead – in the vein of 'Lucky Man'. Emerson remembers that, 'Greg sang it live with just an acoustic guitar and then I added the keyboard parts'.

The original version can be heard on the *Ride the Tiger* mini album released in 2015. Containing six songs written and recorded by Lake and Downes in 1988, one of which ('Love Under Fire') went on to become an Asia song. 'Affairs of the Heart' on *Ride the Tiger* was slower and a more lush electronic arrangement, brimming with synth layers. ELP would also use one of the other tracks from the project, 'Street War', which appeared on ELP's final studio album, *In the Hot Seat*.

### 'Romeo and Juliet' (Prokofiev, arranged Emerson)

The only classical piece on *Black Moon* is an adaption of the instantly recognisable 'Dance of the Knights' – from Prokofiev's *Romeo and Juliet* ballet. After noticing its startling similarity to 'Purple Haze', Emerson said that he attacked the piece in the spirit of Hendrix – full-throttled and boisterous. Lake and Palmer play a shuffle, similar to that on 'Fanfare for the Common Man', allowing the track to motor nicely, neatly avoiding the trap of it becoming a lame 'rock does the classics' pastiche. 'Romeo and Juliet' was especially effective live, as evidenced by the band's slick performance captured on *Live at the Royal Albert Hall*.

'Romeo and Juliet' is one of the three tracks on *Black Moon* that originates from Emerson's solo project. Its original title was 'Montagues and Capulets'. If anything the earlier Emerson solo version is even better than ELP's, with muscular electric guitar work from Tim Pierce, the guitarist who later lent his playing to the new tracks on *Return of the Manticore*.

### 'Farewell to Arms' (Emerson, Lake)

Lake's lyrical themes often portray him as a thoughtful man and 'Farewell to Arms' is a typical example. Another track written in the shadow of the Gulf War, the words are a call for peace – a plea for mankind to stop making war. In many ways, 'Farewell to Arms' is reminiscent of the tracks on *Emerson, Lake and Powell*, but it never seems to quite catch fire. Lake's half-talking vocal style makes the song sound ponderous, almost as if he is trying too hard to convey the serious meaning behind his words. Backed by Emerson's hybrid wurlitzer-come-church-organ (a strange combination in itself) and Palmer's rather simplistic reverb-drenched drumming, the track drags. Emerson attempts to lift the track towards the end with a 'Lucky Man' style synth solo, but devoid of the full-throated bombast of his Moog, it flounders and fades.

Victory chose to issue 'Farewell to Arms' as a promo-only CD single in Germany – complete with a unique triple gatefold sleeve. Coming only two years after German reunification in 1990 and only a year after the German rock band Scorpions had a massive worldwide hit with 'Wind of Change', one can only assume Victory were priming German radio stations with ELP's anti-war anthem. However, the stations didn't take the bait and 'Farewell to Arms' stayed as an album track only.

## 'Changing States' (Emerson)

The second track that was originally destined for Emerson's solo album is 'Changing States' – or as it was previously called, 'Another Frontier'. As with 'Romeo and Juliet', the original Emerson version sounds much stronger, benefitting from a more upfront and less glossy production. ELP's 'Changing States' was also a full minute shorter and had a less progressive arrangement with, yet again, Tim Pierce's impressive guitar helping to add some extra oomph. The guys in Emerson's band really sound like they mean it, whereas in comparison, on *Black Moon* it all sounds a bit half-hearted and 'by the numbers'. One can't help think that had Mancina used a similar arrangement to Emerson's original, with a more aggressive production, ELP fans would have lapped it up. It isn't that 'Changing States' is bad; it isn't. Just that once you hear 'Another Frontier', it is hard to go back!

## 'Burning Bridges' (Mancina)

The only Mark Mancina-composed track on *Black Moon*, 'Burning Bridges' is competently played by ELP, to the point there is no immediate indication it isn't a self-composed number. Apparently, Mancina wrote the track specially for the project. In Lake's own words, 'He came in one day and said he'd written a song. We all said it's a great song, let's record it!' Although it is undoubtedly slick, 'Burning Bridges' lacks any personality and is 'off brand' as far as ELP is concerned. We can only surmise on how much the band were being pressurised to write and record material that was radio-friendly during the making of *Black Moon*. Perhaps they were struggling. We know that Emerson was always keen to write longer 'epics' but with no longer songs on the album his comments on having to be held back 'from doing too much' strongly indicate that shorter material was the order of the day.

Mancina's later work on Disney projects contains many echoes of this style of song. Listen, for example, to his collaborations with Elton John on *The Lion King*, or with Phil Collins on *Tarzan*. In commercial terms, it is of course impossible to argue with the success of this kind of material. But was it ELP? Undoubtedly not. Or think of it in another way. Had 'Burning Bridges' managed to get on the soundtrack of a Hollywood movie, would it have kick-started a new direction for ELP and gained the band completely different fanbase? Victory Records wouldn't have complained but it almost doesn't bear thinking about. ELP 'doing a Genesis'? One shudders at the thought!

## 'Close to Home' (Emerson)

The third and final track from Emerson's solo project is 'Close to Home' – a piece he originally titled 'Ballade'. On the *Black Moon* version Lake chose not to emulate the original's acoustic guitar, which had been played by Kevin Gilbert. This is a shame as it would have turned what is essentially just an Emerson solo piano piece into something more collaborative. That said, 'Close to Home' is unmistakably Emerson and an extremely pleasant interlude from the studio production bombast of the rest of the album. No ELP fan is ever going to complain at hearing this kind of material.

## 'Better Days' (Emerson, Lake)
When asked about his lyrics to 'Better Days', Lake's response was, 'It's almost abstract in a way and very dream-like. I couldn't tell you what it's about!' Much of what he wrote about was taken from snatches of observed themes , which he had a knack of turning into memorable songs. As is the case here. On this jointly-written track with Emerson, specially written for *Black Moon*, the band sound a lot more at home than they do on 'Burning Bridges'. Emerson excels on Hammond, which is wonderful to hear after the GX-1-heavy *Works* and *Love Beach*. We even get a brief snatch of what sounds like a Moog, although possibly a patch on one of his new Korgs. It is also great to hear Palmer drumming creatively, as he plays a hypnotic Bodhrán-like pattern, that for some reason brings to mind slapped bass – which was very much in vogue at the time. If there's any criticism, Emerson's keyboards are awash with reverb – a particularly irritating production style of the era.

## 'Footsteps in the Snow' (Lake)
In a low key end to the album, this thoughtful acoustic guitar ballad benefits from some beautifully spacey synth layers from Emerson. And in a style reminiscent of ELP's early albums, Lake's bass playing is pleasingly audible in the mix, his deep, resonant vocals rising above the strummed guitar. According to Lake, 'The whole concept of leaving footsteps in snow is about what you leave behind you, as a memory'. In light of both Keith Emerson and Greg Lake passing away in 2016, 'Footsteps in the Snow' is extremely poignant – an unwitting self-penned tribute to their musical legacy. ELP fans will forever be grateful for the 'Footsteps in the Snow' that both musicians left behind.

## The *Black Moon* Rough Mixes
When *Black Moon* was released, Mancina's production sounded fresh, adding a new slant to ELP's music. What is interesting, is a CD called *Black Moon Rough Mixes*, a release only available to those who bought 2017's *Fanfare 1970-1997* box set via Pledge Music. Containing early mixes of *Black Moon*, dating from December 1991, these less-polished tracks are without the cinematic sheen added by Mancina during the album's final production. They make compelling listening, a glimpse of what might have been had someone else other than Mancina been at the desk.

## Keith Emerson *Changing States*
All ELP fans should hear Emerson's *Changing States* album – his pre-*Black Moon* project which finally saw a release on CD in 1995. Whilst the solo album's *Changing States* title rather confusingly seems to have been taken

from the *Black Moon* track of the same name, the very same instrumental on *Changing States* is called 'Another Frontier'. Worse, on the *Black Moon Rough Mixes* album mentioned above, the track is called 'Frontiers'!

## *Black Moon* rarities and bonus tracks

1992 Sanctuary Records Japanese edition
Serial number: VICP-5164
Only the Japanese edition of *Black Moon* had a bonus track, 'A Blade of Grass', a delicate Emerson piano piece.

1992 Black Moon CD single
Serial number: 869 737-2
This is a noticeably different, more contemporary mix of *Black Moon*. Also included is 'A Blade of Grass' – which was only on the Japanese issue of the album – plus the full album version of 'Black Moon'.

1992 Black Moon 12' single
Serial number: LONX 320
A-side is the 'Black Moon' single mix plus 'A Blade of Grass', with the full album version on the B-side.

1992 Black Moon 7' single
Serial number: LC 0016
A-side is the 'Black Moon' single mix, with the full album version on the B-side.

2001 UK Castle Music reissue
Serial number: CMRCD227
Four bonus tracks are included, the original single version of 'Black Moon', plus edits – seemingly just cut down versions of the album tracks – of 'Affairs of the Heart', 'Paper Blood' and 'Romeo and Juliet'. It also comes with a six-panel double-sided insert with an essay by long time ELP advocate, Chris Welch.

2008 US Shout! Factory reissue
Serial number: 826663-10845
This remastered issue features 'A Blade of Grass', as a bonus track.

2011 UK Sony / Legacy reissue
Serial number: 88697848682
Bonus tracks as per the 2001 Castle Music reissue, plus a Malcom Dome essay on the making of 'Black Moon', in an 8-page booklet.

2017 BMG Deluxe reissue
Serial number: BMGCAT2CD11

Once again, this includes the single version of 'Black Moon' plus the edited versions of 'Affairs of the Heart', 'Paper Blood' and 'Romeo and Juliet'. On a second CD, is a remastered edition of the band's *Live at The Royal Albert Hall*. Rather bizarrely, this 'deluxe' edition omits 'A Blade of Grass', the Emerson piano piece that graced the original Japanese issue of the album. The accompanying booklet does however contain an updated Chris Welch easy and a dedication to Keith Emerson and Greg Lake.

2017 Black Moon Rough Mixes
Serial number: BMGCAT138CD
This previously unreleased album of *Black Moon, The Rough Mixes*, was exclusive to fans who pre-ordered the band's *Fanfare 1970-1997* box set via Pledge Music. The album contains nine tracks, omitting only 'Footsteps in the Snow' from the original album. In addition, what ended up being named 'Changing States' on *Black Moon* has here been retitled 'Frontiers' – presumably in reference to 'Another Frontier' on Emerson's *Changing States* solo album. Essentially, they are all the same track!

# In the Hot Seat (1994)

Personnel:

Keith Emerson: keyboards & keyboard programming (assisted by Keith Wechsler, Richard Baker & Brain Foraker)

Greg Lake: vocals, bass, guitar

Carl Palmer: drums (additional drum programming by Keith Wechsler)

Additional musicians:

Background vocals: Bill Wray & Paula Mattioli

Choir on *Pictures at an Exhibition* Fred White, Ricky Nelson, Lynn B Davis, Linda McCrary

Released: 27 September 1994

Recorded: Goodnight LA Studios, California

Producer: Keith Olsen

Engineered: Brian Foraker & Keith Olsen

After the critical success of *Black Moon* and the extended world tour that followed, ELP were keen to keep up momentum and release their second album of the Nineties. However, disaster struck when Keith Emerson began to notice a problem with the fingers on his right hand. He was forced to undergo surgery and by the time the band started record *Black Moon*'s follow up – initially titled *The Best in The House* – his hand still hadn't fully recovered. Worse was to come, when Carl Palmer began to suffer carpal tunnel syndrome after noticing a numbness in his fingers. Emerson readily admitted, 'It was a tough time to make an album'.

Greg Lake was reticent for another reason – the decision to use Keith Olson as producer, complete with a series of guest musicians and writers to help bolster the sound. The pressure to emulate the success of ELP's former prog rock contemporaries, Genesis, was both unbearable and totally unrealistic. ELP's label, Victory, were increasingly desperate for a hit record – especially after Bowie's group project, Tin Machine, and the label's other heavyweight progressive rock band, Yes, had both failed to deliver. In dire financial straits, the onus was on ELP to save the day.

Olsen was known to the band as he had produced their new tracks on 1993's *Return of the Manticore* box set. The sessions were a success – including their only full studio recording of *Pictures at an Exhibition* – but the situation was now very different. For the new album, not only did ELP have to write new material, they also had to contend with the injuries to two of the three band members. Throughout the '70s and '80s, and well into the 1990s, Olsen had built a reputation as a producer of note. With more than 39 gold, 24 platinum, and 14 multi-platinum albums to his credit, on paper he seemed more than up to the job. And, to be fair to ELP and Olson, the album they went on to make is by no means the total disaster it is generally made out to be by many fans. As Lake said, 'When you look back on it now, there are some very good elements.' He went on to say, 'He was a great producer, although I'd say that 90 per cent of the record was made individually, without the band playing together. It was very much a constructed record – which was a strange experience for us. It resulted in a different type of record and not one that I would have chosen. I'm more a band guy!'

Although Palmer fully recovered after surgery, in the studio sessions Emerson had to resort to overdubbing his right hand parts using his left hand. Unable to play to the high standard he demanded of himself, it is no surprise that his mental state began to suffer. One can only imagine the tensions around the band at this difficult time. ELP were also desperately short of material – and what material they did have, they were unable to play to their satisfaction. Although modern studio production techniques would have meant this made little difference to many other bands, to ELP, who were used to playing live in the studio, the situation was critical. Olsen received four joint writing credits – a strong indication of his careful nurturing of Lake and Emerson's fledgling song ideas. Palmer received no credits whatsoever. On previous ELP albums, a Palmer credit usually shows that the track in question had been played or jammed live before recording. Lake later confessed that all of the tracks were constructed in the studio, piece by piece.

There are also rumours that many of the parts were played by session musicians. Certainly, several of the keyboard parts are far too repetitive to have been played by Emerson. The same goes for the drums, which are mechanical and very unlike the kind of patterns Palmer would play. When *In the Hot Seat,* was recorded, copy and paste editing techniques – no doubt the reason behind the repetition – were very much the norm in sound studios. The way ELP did things in their heyday, by playing live in the studio, had changed beyond all recognition. Thus, regardless of the medical condition of Emerson and Palmer, this could well have been the way the album was created anyway. That said, by refusing to let ELP be the band they wanted to be, it was never going to end well.

To nobody's surprise, the album was both a critical and commercial flop. It is by far the worst selling ELP album. Listening to *In the Hot Seat* again today, it is by no means the impossible listen most would have you believe. It could have been a lot better of course – but it could also have been a lot worse. The burning question among fans is whether *In the Hot Seat* is better or worse than *Love Beach*? I'll leave it to you to decide.

## 'Hand of Truth' (Emerson, Lake)

One of ELPs best post-*Works* tracks, it is a shame that this promising start to the *In the Hot Seat* wasn't fully capitalised upon. From the opening chords, this is the sound of a modern day ELP. But it is an all too brief taste of what could have been. Originally titled 'We Have the Power', Lake's lyrics tackle the thorny subject of the environment in a concise mini-epic, jam packed with all of the hallmarks of a classic ELP track. Despite Emerson's hand problems he performs a wonderful Moog-style solo at the end – one of the few solos on the entire album. Apparently, he had to have several takes and one can only imagine the mental and physical pain this took. Listening to 'Hand of Truth', one can hear the 'cut and paste' studio editing needed to piece together the keyboard parts. And, if the rumours are true, some passages weren't even played by Emerson at all.

The song's weighty subject matter brings to mind something Carl Palmer said in a 1995 interview – that ELP's next album (which turned out to be *In the Hot Seat*) was going to be a concept on global issues both 'political and topical'. Although Lake's lyrics on 'Hand of Truth' are at times rather awkward and clichéd, the band's desire to tackle issues away from their more traditional dystopian sci-fi theme is good to hear. It is known that ELP entered the studio with a few tracks already prepared. Can we assume 'The Hand of Truth' was one of them?

## 'Daddy' (Lake)

Inspired to write this heartfelt song after watching the US TV show, *America's Most Wanted*, Lake became greatly affected by the case of a missing young girl, Sara Anne Wood. ''Daddy' is one of the most important tracks for me on the whole album. To be honest, 'Daddy' is not much of a song, except it has a lot of meaning for me. It is a story about a child who had been abducted and murdered.' He went on to say that, 'I had a daughter of my own and could not imagine what her father, Robert, must have suffered. He carried on his search for her in upstate New York with a party of volunteers in sub-zero temperatures, I remember watching this interview on TV and somebody said to him, 'How on earth do you manage to keep going in these conditions?' He just looked up and said, 'I can hear her calling me. She'd say, Daddy come and bring me home'. That did it, I had to write the song as a way of getting it out of my psyche'.

Lake went on to meet the girl's father, Robert Wood, after writing him a moving letter. Royalties from 'Daddy' were donated to the foundation for missing children set up in Sara Anne Wood's memory. Lake went on to make several appearances on TV to promote both the track and the charity. It is hard not to be moved by Lake's lyrics and it is a credit that not only did he tackle such an emotive subject but that he carried it off with such heartfelt aplomb. The girl's voice on the track was provided by Olsen's own daughter, Kristen.

If there is any criticism, it is that the track is so strong in terms of its heartfelt theme, it sits uneasily within the context of the album. Any pace and structure that might have otherwise existed, flowing from 'Hand of Truth' to 'One by One' is destroyed. One cannot help wonder whether 'Daddy' would have been better left off the album and issued as a charity single instead.

## 'One by One' (Emerson, Lake, Olsen)

From the off, again this is unmistakably ELP, Olsen gaining a deserved credit for marshalling ELP's signature sound into a concise 3 minutes and 20 seconds. With piano, Moog-esque synths and even some Hammond, it sounds as if Emerson may be playing live, at least, far more than he does on 'Hand of Truth'. Although the orchestral synth stabs now sound dated, they don't detract from Lake's strong vocals, even if the lyrics are sometimes vague and mawkish. Palmer's drums arrive late to the party, muffling the drum machine hi-hat after the first chorus. Why anyone would use a drum machine when you have a drummer of Palmer's calibre on hand beggars belief. The only explanation I can think of is that Olsen was pandering to pop music fashion and attempting to add a contemporary touch. Which is fair enough, but when creating an ELP album one can't help but think this is tantamount to treason!

The track ends with a valiant attempt to circumnavigate Emerson's hand problem by using a repeating synth figure. This actually works really well, possibly more so than had Emerson been allowed to overindulge himself with a complicated solo. All in all, a decent enough track that doesn't do anything to embarrass ELP's legacy.

## 'Heart on Ice' (Lake, Olsen)

Olsen again gets a co-credit in this rather forgettable syrupy ballad. Despite being backed by some assured Emerson piano, Lake's vocal lines never grab the attention, with a melody line and lyrics that sound unconvincing. Listen instead to Palmer's drums, which in production terms sound way better than they ever did on *Black Moon*, with crisp cymbals, a deep snare and an audible kick. Palmer really excels in this masterclass of restrained drumming, making every hit count. Lake later commented that he wasn't happy with Olsen's production of the track but it is hard to hear what irked him. Perhaps it was the unnecessary use of synth strings in the intro? Overall though, the track's failing has more to do with the lack of a memorable vocal melody than anything else. That and the fact this isn't really ELP but more a second-rate Lake solo track.

## 'Thin Line' (Wary, Olsen, Emerson)

If 'Heart on Ice' isn't the true sound of ELP, then 'Thin Line' is something else entirely! It isn't as if this is a bad song, far from it, it is just that this kind of song has little business on an ELP album. It is perhaps telling that Emerson's name appears last on the credits, as if he was given a belated but deferential nod for adding in some growling Hammond – which sounds great by the way. And it isn't as if Lake shouldn't be singing this kind of material either, as he makes a pretty good fist of it. The problem is that the sound of 'Thin Line' could be any number of generic American rock bands of the era. Again, looking at the positives, Palmer's drumming is excellent. To be fair, whoever plays the guitar (it doesn't sound at all like Lake), is more than competent but an American hard rock sound is out of place on an ELP album. Halfway through the track, Emerson takes a welcome Hammond solo but he is inexplicably backed by an electric guitar in full whammy-mode. Who ever thought that was a good idea? It can't be denied that this all very slick – and once again it isn't hard to imagine it on the soundtrack for any number of 1990s Hollywood movies – but it just isn't ELP.

### 'Man in the Long Black Coat' (Dylan, arranged Emerson)

'Man in the Long Black Coat' is the only time ELP ever covered one of Dylan's songs. The track originally appeared on the 1989's *Oh Mercy* album, produced by Daniel Lanois. Bearing in mind Lake's first solo album featured a song proudly co-written with Dylan – making him is the only male songwriter to have ever got a co-writing credit – and that The Nice covered covered three of Dylan's songs ('Country Pie', 'My Back Pages' and 'She Belongs to Me'), this is something of a surprise. Palmer later said that Emerson wanted to use 'Man in the Long Black Coat' as the basis for a longer concept piece, 'a kind of Western with a screenplay written by Dylan'. Sadly, the idea never came to fruition as Olsen wasn't at all keen on the idea. Lake and Palmer were also concerned that Dylan would get the bulk of the writing credit despite the band putting in a great deal of effort to arrange and orchestrate it. Thankfully, Emerson's work didn't go to waste as it ended up as the core of 'One by One'.

With the wind taken out of his sails, it isn't surprising that Emerson's arrangement of 'Man in the Long Black Coat' is somewhat lacklustre. It is slightly reminiscent of the tracks on *Emerson, Lake & Powell,* perhaps because of the style of Lake's vocal delivery. The track is played straight, with only a hint of a keyboard solo at the very beginning and again at the end. Had Emerson been match fit, the solos would almost certainly have been expanded on, even under Olsen's cosh! To gain some perspective, one should listen to the original, Lanois' lush production conveying a sense of atmosphere that ELP's version doesn't come close to achieving. We can chalk this one up as a missed opportunity.

### 'Change' (Wray, Emerson, Olsen)

A weak 'by numbers' song, Lake's vocals sound unsure throughout, despite his professional delivery. It is difficult to hear any Emerson influence on 'Change', leaving one to wonder how he gained a co-writing credit. Once again Palmer excels, his tenure in Asia playing more straightforward rhythms paying dividends. That aside, there really isn't anything to warrant commenting on. It even sounds as if even Olsen had lost interest by this point.

### 'Give Me a Reason to Stay' (Diamond, Lorber)

Written specially for Lake's rich voice by the songwriters Steve Diamond and Sam Lorber, at best this sounds an outtake. Halfway through, an electric guitar takes a solo – played in an anthemic rock style that doesn't remotely sound like Lake's playing. The piano at this point doesn't sound like Emerson either. All Lake would say on the track is that, 'I was the interpreter'. Which is polite way of saying he sang someone else's song and has zero feelings on anything else. We're left wondering why half-baked songs like this were being used to hammer nails into ELP's once proud legacy.

## 'Gone Too Soon' (Lake, Wray, Weehsler)

Is this the sound of ELP doing Genesis? Neither Emerson nor Palmer feature on the track, which is a shame as it is an otherwise pleasant uptempo song that could potentially have been a hit. The keyboards and guitars are played by unnamed session musicians. Even worse, the percussion is provided by a drum machine. ELP frequently declined to comment on the track, Lake only saying, 'I have to be honest, I can't even remember the thing!' If there was a song on the album that could have done something in terms of the singles chart, this is the one. A shame then that EL and P weren't allowed to sink their collective teeth into it to give it the magic needed to make it a cut above the rest.

## 'Street War' (Emerson, Lake)

From Lake's *Ride the Tiger* project with Geoff Downes – which he said he much preferred to the version here – this is a song about the onset of terrorism. Lake admits that he didn't fully capture the nub of the subject but said he really liked the song. Oddly, despite it originally being jointly credited to Downes and Lake (when it appeared on the *Ride the Tiger* album), on the credits to *In the Hot Seat*, Lake's name was only joined by Emerson's. With some luck it could have been a minor hit or even graced the soundtrack of a *Miami Vice* style movie!

## 'Pictures at an Exhibition'

A. **'Promenade'** (Mussorgsky, arranged Emerson)

B. **The Gnome** (Mussorgsky, arranged Palmer)

C. **'Promenade'** (Mussorgsky, Lake)

D. **The Sage** (Lake)

E. **'The Hut Of Baba Yaga'** (Mussorgsky, arranged Emerson)

F. **The Great Gates of Kiev** (Mussorgsky, Lake, arranged Emerson)

This new version of *Pictures at an Exhibition* was originally recorded, with Olsen in the production chair, for ELP's *Return of the Manticore* box set. Because the box set was regarded as a niche purchase, the decision was made to issue it again, as a 'bonus track' on *In the Hot Seat*. Aside from an early version of 'Promenade' from 1970, which had been included on 2012's reissue of ELP's first album, this is the only time the band ever tackled *Pictures at an Exhibition* in the studio. The success of the recording is one of the reasons that led to Olsen being chosen as producer for *In the Hot Seat*.

Recorded with the help of a gospel choir, *Pictures at an Exhibition* was recorded with the ground-breaking Dolby Surround Sound technology –

something the band were very taken with at the time. According to Palmer, 'We only ever recorded *Pictures* live and never had the opportunity to record it in a controlled situation. The new version adds a lot more dynamics. We've not only done justice to the piece, we've given it a new life!' Lake was similarly enthused, 'For a long time we've wanted to make a studio version of *Pictures at an Exhibition*. We'd done a live broadcast in Dolby Surround Sound and were talking about a future album co-operation, so we seized that opportunity to use it for the box set.'

This new recording of *Pictures* is extremely impressive and is worth buying *In the Hot Seat* for its inclusion alone. Recorded before Emerson began to experience problems with his hand, his playing is imaginative and precise, breathing new life into the piece. Olsen's presence here is a boon, the band free of the restraints he applied during the making *In the Hot Seat*. Both the production and the band's playing give *Pictures at an Exhibition* a contemporary cinematic sheen. For fans, it is like hearing the piece afresh. Emerson chooses to eschew his Hammond for large parts of the recording, favouring polyphonic synthesisers instead. Whereas, in the days of his GX-1, this could have created a rather bland soundscape, here it works effectively, orchestrating Mussorgsky's original composition to great effect. Lake's 'The Sage' is similarly impressive – although his voice sounds strained, the effect of years of touring and heavy smoking taking its inevitable toll. Perhaps wisely, Lake chose not to emulate the fast acoustic guitar picking on the original, instead taking a couple of short tasteful solos sensitively backed by Emerson. 'The Great Gates of Kiev' is another triumph, the use of a gospel choir at the finale sending chills up your spine. Although not as iconic as the band's original live recording, this new version of *Pictures at an Exhibition* is nonetheless an essential listen for any ELP fan. And bearing in mind it was recorded only a year or so before *In the Hot Seat* makes it all the more bewildering and sad they weren't given the chance to follow it up with a brand new set of recordings in true ELP style.

## *In the Hot Seat* rarities and bonus tracks

2010 Japanese edition
Serial number: VICP-70162 (reissued in 2012 as VICP-75071 and in 2015 as VICP-78040)
Housed in a cardboard sleeve and with a traditional Japanese 'obi' stripe this unique version included Emerson's 'Hammer it Out' as a bonus track. 'Hammer it Out' is more commonly available on Emerson's 2002 jazz / classical album of piano pieces, *Emerson Plays Emerson*. It was also later issued as part of his 2005 double CD anthology album, *Hammer it Out*.

201& BMG deluxe edition
Serial number: BMGCAT2CD12

Squeezed on to the end of the first CD and spread across the entire second CD, this remastered 'deluxe' edition includes the band's live recordings from their *Now Tour* '87 / '98. This is the same but remastered version of their *Then & Now* CD minus the three tracks from 1974's California Jam.

201& BMG / Manticore vinyl edition
Serial number: BMGCATLP12
As part of the revival of the Manticore label, most of ELP's albums were re-issued on vinyl. For *In the Hot Seat,* however, this release marked the first and only time it has been pressed on vinyl.

# ELP Live Albums

Listed below, are ELP's essential live albums, covering the entire spectrum of their career, from their second gig at 1970's Isle of Wight Festival, to their final performance at the High Voltage Festival in London on 25 July 2010. In between, they toured with Quadraphonic sound systems, elevating grand pianos, rotating drum kits, Persian carpets, foam-firing armadillos, antique brass cannons and rather infamously, a 70-piece orchestra. The orchestra – and its financial aftermath – caused a festering rift that eventually split the band in the aftermath of *Love Beach*. Burnt out and jaded, the three members started to fade away into relative obscurity, a far cry from their god-like fame in the Seventies.

Holed beneath the waterline, damaged by punk's angry broadsides and the trio's own rampant egos, nobody thought ELP would ever reform. But they did, re-energised and raring to go in the early-90s. Seemingly putting all their problems behind them, they embarked on a series of world tours, the first of which brought them back to the UK, including three nights at London's Royal Albert Hall – a venue Keith Emerson had previously been banned from. ELP continued to tour throughout the '90s, performing many tracks they'd ignored in their Seventies heyday – much to the delight of fans. After disbanding again at the end of the '90s, ELP returned for one last gig to celebrate their 40th Anniversary, a triumphant headline performance in London at 2010's High Voltage Festival. Sadly, it was to be their last gig.

Although the show was finally over, they left a magnificent legacy of live material that is crying out to be explored and re-evaluated. Never forget that at heart, ELP were a live band, thriving on stage in a heady mix of showmanship and dazzling improvisation. From ambitious progressive masterpieces such as *Tarkus* to Greg Lake's easy-on-the-ear acoustic ballads, it is all here to be enjoyed … again and again.

Note that in brackets are the dates of each release, not the date of the recording. For recording dates please read the text.

## Welcome Back, My Friends, to the Show That Never Ends ~ Ladies and Gentlemen (1974)

ELP's best known live album, *Welcome Back, My Friends, to the Show That Never Ends ~ Ladies and Gentlemen* was recorded at the peak of their fame, towards the end of the *Brain Salad Surgery* tour in August 1974. In true ELP fashion it was housed in an opulent triple gatefold sleeve, each of the three vinyl albums held in E, L and P shaped pockets. It reached number 6 in the UK charts and number 4 on the Billboard 200 – an incredible achievement for a triple album.

Recorded on 24-track tape using a 40-channel mixing desk, *Welcome Back* was originally planned for a Quadraphonic release but problems with the vinyl mastering process led to the project being cancelled. A Quadraphonic mix did however get released on 8-track cartridge. This is a very collectible item for

ELP fans today, although sourcing a copy may be easier than finding a working Quadraphonic 8-track player! ELP's PA system on the *Brain Salad Surgery* tour was Quadraphonic, which explains why they were so keen for those who bought the album to experience the sound as heard at their gigs. One wonders whether the Quad masters still exist. If they do, they'd make an excellent basis for a 5.1 surround sound issue, *Welcome Back* having never received the deluxe reissue treatment... yet.

Before *Welcome Back* was originally released, some of the tracks were broadcast on the American rock music radio show, The King Biscuit Flower Hour. Although taken from the same masters, these were a completely different mix. A CD of these mixes was released in 1997 as *King Biscuit Flower Hour*, which compiled the 1974 gig with those of a much later *Works*-era King Biscuit Flower Hour performance.

## In Concert (1979)

Released after ELP had announced their break up, post-*Love Beach*, *In Concert* is the name of the original vinyl album that includes live tracks from their legendary 1977 concert at the Olympic Stadium in Montreal. It was later re-issued on CD, in an expanded format, as *Works Live*. For the vinyl release, no producer was credited on the sleeve – despite all production and mixing having been overseen by Keith Emerson. Emerson had wanted to release *In Concert* as a double album but because ELP had already broken up, Atlantic restricted it to a single LP.

## Live at the Royal Albert Hall (1993)

Recorded on the *Black Moon* tour, after ELP had reformed, *Live at the Royal Albert Hall* documents an ELP performance at the Royal Albert Hall on 3 October 1993 – one of three nights they played at the famous London venue. The gig was also released on videotape, and later on DVD.

## Live at the Isle of Wight, 1970 (1997)

The band had only been existence for around six weeks when they played only their second ever gig, at the legendary 1970 Isle of Wight Festival. At this point, their debut album had yet to be recorded, let alone released, so the audience were extremely unfamiliar with the material they performed – apart from *Rondo,* which Keith Emerson had promised The Nice fans he'd continue to play with his new band. It is after seeing ELP at the festival, that BBC DJ John Peel infamously called them 'a tragic waste of time, talent and electricity'. But what did he know eh?

## King Biscuit Flower Hour (1997)

Released in 1997, this CD features ELP's two King Biscuit Flower Hour performances – from 1974 and 1977. The tracks from the earlier gig were remixed and issued on *Welcome Back, My Friends, to the Show That Never Ends ~ Ladies and Gentlemen.* Fans will note that despite the tracks originating from the same master tapes, they have completely different mixes. Many fans prefer the King Biscuit Flower Hour mix, making this album an essential purchase.

### Live in Poland (1997)
Recorded in Katowice in June 1997, this was originally an exclusive Poland-only release. The ELP gigs on this tour are notable for a 'Pictures at an Exhibition' / 'Tarkus' medley, which is featured here in its entirety. Interestingly, the only track missing from the band's performance that night is 'Tiger in a Spotlight', which preceded 'Touch and Go' in the set list.

### Then and Now (1998)
An eclectic but nonetheless fascinating release, housed in a Giger cover! *Then and Now* features recordings from ELP's 97/98 tour plus three tracks from their iconic 1974 California Jam performance. All of the 1974 tracks here would later appear on 2012's *Live in California*. Among the later tracks from 97/98 is 'Touch and Go' – originally recorded on the Emerson, Lake & Powell album. The album's sleeve notes dedicate ELP's live version here to Cozy Powell, who had lost his life in a car accident in April 1998.

### The Original Bootleg Series from the Manticore Vaults (2001 - 2006)
An extensive four-volume series, featuring a total of 28 CDs, covering ELP's live performances from 1971 to 1993. The idea behind these beautifully-presented sets is to beat the bootleggers at their own game. Remastered from a variety of sound sources, the quality varies from excellent to mediocre but all manage to capture the spirit of attending an ELP gig. Some of the performances are absolutely incendiary, making you wish the band had recorded them properly. That said, we should be grateful for their existence at all! Each concert comes in its own miniature sleeve, designed to emulate the charm of the vinyl bootleg era. Definitely one for die-hard fans but a rewarding listening experience for those who wish to dig deeper.

### High Voltage Festival (2010)
A double CD of ELP's final concert at the High Voltage Festival in London on 25 July, 2010. The performance was also released on DVD. Worth owning for sentimental value alone.

### Live at the Mar Y Sol festival '72 (2011)
A must-own live set from 1972 that features gritty versions of early ELP classics, including a cut-down performance of 'Pictures at an Exhibition'. For a long

time, the only way to hear ELP's performance from Mar Y Sol was two tracks –'Take A Pebble' and' 'Tank'– included on a 1972 double live vinyl LP featuring a selection of artists from the festival. However, the discovery of the original 16-track master tapes of the gig inspired their inclusion in 2007's *From the Beginning* box set. This stand-alone CD replicates those tracks. Lastly, as part of 2011's Record Store Day in the UK, 'Pictures at an Exhibition' and 'Tarkus' from the festival were compiled to create *Mar Y Sol,* a unique limited edition (1,500 copies) vinyl album.

## Live at Nassau Coliseum '78 (2011)

On the *Works* tour, after the orchestra had been laid off due to impending financial disaster, the band performed all remaining dates as a trio. This 1978 performance is an excellent example of how their sound became rawer as a result. In many ways, this is the perfect antidote to the more polished sound on *Works Live*. It features several tracks not featured on that release, 'Tarkus' being the most notable. It is worth hearing for the cheeky musical references Emerson throws in during 'Aquatarkus' – brief snippets from Hollywood blockbuster movies of the time, such as *Star Wars* and *Close Encounters.*

## Live in California 1974 (2012)

For many years, a recording of ELP's iconic performance at the California Jam was considered the Holy Grail for fans. This 2012 release gathers together all known surviving ELP audio of this historic gig. Some tracks are incomplete, whilst a couple are missing. For example, neither 'Tarkus' nor 'Jerusalem', both of which were played on the night, are represented here. It is, however, an invaluable record of ELP playing live at the pinnacle of their career. Note that the film footage that originally accompanied this audio is featured on the band's 2005 *Beyond the Beginning* DVD.

## Live in Montreal 1977 (2013)

For the first time, this release gathers together all surviving audio from ELP's Olympic Stadium performance on 26 August 1977. The only two tracks missing are 'Hoedown' and 'Tarkus', neither of which could be salvaged from the master tapes. New to this release are 'Karn Evil 9, First Impression Part 2', 'Lucky Man', 'Nutrocker' and 'Pirates'. All other tracks were previously available on *Works Live*.

## Once Upon a Time in South America (2015)

This four CD set, from the band's 1993 world tour, was recorded live at Estadio Chile, Santiago on 1 April, Obras Stadium, Buenos Aires on 5 April 5, and the Metropolitan Theater, Rio de Janeiro on 16 August. The tour is notable for ELP's live performance of King Crimson's '21st Century Schzoid Man' – which is featured here. A double vinyl album was also released, featuring a compilation of the tracks from the more comprehensive CD set.

## Live at Montreux 1997 (2015)

Originally released as a DVD, the audio of this 1997 gig was released as a double CD in 2015. A double vinyl edition was released in 2016 as part of Record Store Day in the UK.

# ELP collaborations and solo albums

The following is a list of the various post-ELP solo albums and projects involving Keith Emerson, Greg Lake and Carl Palmer. Just two of these have been expanded on because of their significance to ELP's recording history – 1986's *Emerson, Lake & Powell* and 3's *To the Power of Three* from 1988.

## Emerson Lake & Powell (1986)

Personnel:
Keith Emerson: keyboards
Greg Lake: vocals, bass & guitars
Cozy Powell: drums & percussion.
Released: 26 May 1986
Recorded: Maison Rouge, London and Fleetwood Mobile, East Sussex.
Produced: Tony Taverner & Greg Lake
Highest chart place: 35 in UK, 23 US Billboard 200

In the aftermath of ELP disbanding at the end of 1979, all three members were soon busy on various projects. Keith Emerson busied himself with film scores and recorded a rather patchy solo album, *Honky*, in 1981. Greg Lake recorded two solo albums and toured with a band that included Gary Moore on guitar. Carl Palmer formed the AOR band 1PM, releasing one album, before he became a founder member of Asia – by far the most successful progressive / AOR band of the era. Asia achieved what ELP could not, having hit singles – notably 'Heat of the Moment', which reached number four in the US Billboard Hot 100. Impressively, it stayed at number one in the Billboard Mainstream Rock chart for six consecutive weeks. Asia's debut album has sold around ten million copies worldwide. Lake, rather infamously, joined Asia, on a temporary basis, in 1983. This was after singer/bassist John Wetton left the group before a high profile gig at the Budokan Hall in Japan. The first ever concert to be broadcast live via satellite, it was an important moment for the group, Palmer convincing Lake to help them out at extremely short notice.

Due to Asia's continuing success, when Emerson and Lake discussed getting ELP back together in 1985, Palmer was unavailable. After auditions, they decided on veteran rock drummer Cozy Powell. The P of his surname allowed the band to keep the ELP moniker, although they've always insisted his surname was a pure coincidence. The album they recorded, the eponymously titled *Emerson, Lake & Powell*, was firmly in the ELP style. A vast improvement on *Love Beach*, it included the single 'Touch & Go', a track that would later find its way into ELP's setlist when they reformed in the early-1990s. Sadly, Emerson, Lake & Powell toured just once, in support of their album, splitting before they could record a follow up. An album of the band in rehearsal, *The Sprocket Sessions*, was made available after it had been widely bootlegged. 'Touch & Go' was re-recorded by ELP for their 1993

*Return of the Manticore* box set.

Emerson, Lake & Powell's live shows were well received, perhaps inevitably including a majority of ELP pieces. A retrospective live album was released in 2003 and included 'Tank, 'Pirates', 'From the Beginning', 'Lucky Man', 'Fanfare for the Common Man' and 'Karn Evil 9 1st Impression'.

# To the Power of Three (1988)

Personnel:
Keith Emerson: Keyboards
Robert Berry: vocals, bass & guitars
Carl Palmer: drums & percussion.
Released: 25 March 1988
Recorded: E-Zee Studios & West Side Studios, London
Produced: Carl Palmer & Robert Berry
Chart positions: 97 US Billboard 200

Of all the ELP off-shoot albums, 3's *To the Power of Three,* should arguably have been the biggest success. With both Keith Emerson and Carl Palmer on board – and a fresh young singer, Robert Berry, handling guitar and bass – the template was set for an Eighties reinvention of ELP. Yet despite *To the Power of Three* being highly polished and containing all of the Emerson hallmarks, it failed to ignite. Without a hit single to help promote the album it briefly fizzled and sunk without trace. To their credit, the band toured in April and May 1988 in support of the album – to mostly sold out venues – but with a set list that all but ignored ELP's classics. Emerson realised, too late, that the project had been a mistake. 3's slick and radio-friendly sound simply didn't float Emerson's boat – it wasn't what he wanted at the time – and the band quietly disbanded.

Had 3 been given the chance to shine, they may well have grown to become a band of note. *To the Power of Three,* is unashamedly an album that reeks of 1980s production values but it also sounds like a proper band. And with Berry's unassuming and affable character, there was little danger of a return to the hassles and arguing that had dogged ELP in the *Love Beach* era. In 2017, after Emerson's death, Berry announced he'd been exchanging tapes with Emerson ever since the band split up. They had remained on friendly terms and had a core of material to create a second 3 album. In fact, the two had made plans to record together. A year after Emerson passed away, Berry decided to continue with the album regardless. Entitled *3.2*, it was released in the Summer of 2018 to positive reviews. Emerson was given a co-writing credit on four of the album's eight tracks.

Two live albums of 3 have been released – *Live in Boston '88* and *Live, Rockin' The Ritz*. Both concentrate on 3's own material, although they do include a few ELP tracks. They are well worth hearing.

# Keith Emerson solo albums & projects

## Soundtracks:
*Inferno* (1980)
*Nighthawks* (1981)
*Best Revenge* (1982)
*Murderock* (1983)
*Harmagedon* (1983)
*La Chiesa* (1992)
*Iron Man Volume 1* (2002)

## Solo:
*Honky* (1981)
*The Christmas Album* (1988)
*Changing States* (1995)
*Emerson Plays Emerson* (2002)

## Projects & collaborations:
*Vivacitas, Live at Glasgow* (2002) – with The Nice
*Boys Clubs, Live From California* (2009) – with Glenn Hughes and Marc Bonilla
*Three Fates Project* (2012) – with Terje Mikkelsen and Marc Bonilla
*Live From Manticore Hall* (2014) – with Greg Lake

## Notable compilations:
*At the Movies* (2005)
*Hammer It Out* (2005)
*Off the Shelf* (2006)

# Greg Lake solo albums & projects

## Solo:
*Greg Lake* (1981)
*Manoeuvres* (1983)
*King Biscuit Hour Presents Greg Lake Live* (1995)
*Greg Lake* (2007) – recorded live on Lake's 2005 tour
*Songs of a Lifetime* (2013) – live recording from Lake's *Songs of a Lifetime* tour
*Live in Piacenza* (2017) – live recording from Lake's *Songs of a Lifetime* tour

## Projects & collaborations:
*Live From Manticore Hall* (2014) – with Keith Emerson
*Ride the Tiger* (2015) – with Geoff Downes

**Notable compilations:**
*From The Underground Volume 1* (1998)
*From the Underground Volume 2* (2010)

# Carl Palmer solo albums & projects

## Solo:
*Working Live, Volume 1* (2002)
*Working Live, Volume 2* (2004)
*Working Live, Volume 3* (2010)

## Projects & collaborations:
*1PM* (1980) – with 1PM
*Asia (1982)* – with Asia
*Alpha (1983)* – with Asia
*Astra (1985)* – with Asia
*Aqua (1992)* – with Asia
*Live in the Hood* (2000) – with Qango
*Phoenix (2008)* – with Asia
*Omega (2010)* – with Asia
*XXX (2012)* – with Asia
*Gravitas (2014)* – with Asia

## Notable compilation:
*Do Ya Wanna Play, Carl?* (2001)

# References & bibography

The following websites will cast further light on both ELP and those that have been associated with the band over the years:

emersonlakeplamer.com
keithemerson.com
greglake.com
carlpalmer.com
ladiesofthelake.com
brain-salad-surgery.de
brain-salad.com
marcbonilla.com
robertberry.com
noddyspuncture.co.uk

The following books have been an inspiration and an invaluable source of information. Thanks go to their authors – those who went before me, writing and researching about ELP. All are much recommended, taking the story of ELP far deeper than the scope of this book allows:

Stump, P., *The Music's All That Matters, A History of Progressive Rock* (Quartet Books, 1997)

Emerson, K., *Pictures of an Exhibitionist* (John Blake Publishing, 2004)

Macan, E., *Endless Enigma, A Musical Biography of Emerson, Lake & Palmer (Open Court, 2006)*

*Freeman, G., Do You Wanna Play Some Magic? Emerson, Lake & Palmer in Concert 1970-1979 (Soundcheck Books, 2012)*

Forrester, G., Hanson, M., Askew, F., *Emerson, Lake & Palmer, the show that never ends... encore* (Foruli Classics, 2013)

Lake, G., *Lucky Man, The Autobiography* (Constable, 2017)

# Would you like to write for Sonicbond Publishing?

At Sonicbond Publishing we are always on the look-out for authors, particularly for our two main series:

On Track. Mixing fact with in depth analysis, the On Track series examines the work of a particular musical artist or group. All genres are considered from easy listening and jazz to 60s soul to 90s pop, via rock and metal.

On Screen. This series looks at the world of film and television. Subjects considered include directors, actors and writers, as well as entire television and film series. As with the On Track series, we balance fact with analysis.

While professional writing experience would, of course, be an advantage the most important qualification is to have real enthusiasm and knowledge of your subject. First-time authors are welcomed, but the ability to write well in English is essential.

Sonicbond Publishing has distribution throughout Europe and North America, and all books are also published in E-book form. Authors will be paid a royalty based on sales of their book.

Further details are available from www.sonicbondpublishing.co.uk. To contact us, complete the contact form there or email info@sonicbondpublishing.co.uk

Also from Sonicbond Publishing

**On Track series**
**Deep Purple & Rainbow**
Steve Pilkington ISBN: 978-1-78952-002-6

**Queen**
Andrew Wild ISBN: 978-1-78952-003-3

**Yes**
Stephen Lambe ISBN: 978-1-78952-001-9

**Blue Oyster Cult**
Jacob Holm Lupo ISBN: 978-1-78952-007-1

**The Beatles**
Andrew Wild ISBN: 978-1-78952-009-5

**Roy Wood and the Move**
James R Turner ISBN: 978-1-78952-008-8

**Genesis**
Stuart MacFarlane ISBN: 978-1-78952-005-7

**Jethro Tull**
Jordan Blum ISBN: 978-1-78952-016-3

**The Rolling Stones 1963-80**
Steve Pilkington ISBN: 978-1-78952-017-0

**On Screen series**
**Carry On...**
Stephen Lambe ISBN: 978-1-78952-004-0

**Seinfeld**
Stephen Lambe ISBN: 978-1-78952-012-5

**Audrey Hepburn**
Ellen Cheshire ISBN: 978-1-78952-011-8

**Powell and Pressburger**
Sam Proctor ISBN: 978-1-78952-013-2

**Dad's Army**
Huw Lloyd- Jones ISBN: 978-1-78952-015-6

*and many more to come!*